Understanding
Economic Growth
China in and India

A Comparative Study of Selected Issues

Understanding
Economic Growth
China in and India

A Comparative Study of Selected Issues

Yanrui Wu

University of Western Australia, Australia

World Scientific

NEW JERSEY · LONDON · SINGAPORE · BEIJING · SHANGHAI · HONG KONG · TAIPEI · CHENNAI

CRL
338.951 009051 WU

Published by

World Scientific Publishing Co. Pte. Ltd.

5 Toh Tuck Link, Singapore 596224

USA office: 27 Warren Street, Suite 401-402, Hackensack, NJ 07601

UK office: 57 Shelton Street, Covent Garden, London WC2H 9HE

British Library Cataloguing-in-Publication Data
A catalogue record for this book is available from the British Library.

UNDERSTANDING ECONOMIC GROWTH IN CHINA AND INDIA
A Comparative Study of Selected Issues

ISBN-13 978-981-4287-78-4
ISBN-10 981-4287-78-4

In-house Editor: Wanda Tan

Typeset by Stallion Press
Email: enquiries@stallionpress.com

Printed in Singapore by World Scientific Printers.

Preface

The economies of China and India, the world's two most populous nations, have attracted a lot of attention in recent years. Even a new term, "Chindia", was created to refer to the two countries together in general. There are many comparative studies of the two Asian giants. This volume focuses exclusively on economic growth and several critical issues associated with growth in the two economies. It combines quantitative examination with qualitative analysis. It not only provides valuable insights into those growth-related issues, but also raises many questions which are to be explored in the future. The volume should be of interest to postgraduate students, researchers and business analysts. In particular, the materials in the appendices to some chapters are important resources for other researchers who are interested in the economies of China and India.

My work on this book spans several years. It began with my visit to the East Asian Institute (EAI), at the National University of Singapore (NUS), during my sabbatical leave in 2005; subsequently, I visited EAI several times. I benefited a lot from the library resources at EAI and participation in many seminars and conferences there. Work on some chapters also benefited from the financial support of a University of Western Australia (UWA) Research Grant as well as an Australian Research Council (ARC) Discovery Project Grant (DP1092913). I would also like to thank seminar participants at EAI (NUS), the economics group (UWA), School of Management (University of Bradford), and China

Research Centre (University of Technology, Sydney) for helpful comments and suggestions. I also acknowledge James Tsun Se Cheong, Rebecca Doran-Wu, Hetish Gupta and Nic Yew Sin for their excellent research assistance.

Yanrui Wu
University of Western Australia
Perth, Australia

Contents

List of Tables

List of Figures

Chapter 1

Introduction

High growth in China and India has stimulated a lively debate about economic performance and long-term development in the two Asian giants and, subsequently, the emergence of a literature on the comparison of the two economies.[1] Though some observers have raised the question about the potential competition and hence confrontation between China and India, most authors are merely interested in the contrasts and similarities between economic growth patterns in the two countries. China and India are similar in terms of their level and initial conditions of development, the size of their population and their geographical location (being Asian neighbors). The two nations used to have the world's largest economies, together accounting for about half of the world's output five centuries ago, according to Maddison (2003). This income share was parallel to their population share at that time. Unfortunately, over the past centuries, both economies suffered from long-time stagnation and decline as Western Europe and the US rose in turn during the same period (Figure 1.1). By 1950, about 36% of the world's population lived in China and India, but they accounted for less than 9% of the world's income (Desai, 2003). The relative decline of the economic power of the two nations continued until the late 1970s in China and mid-1980s in India, when economic reforms were initiated in the two economies.

---

[1] See, for example, Huang and Khanna (2003), Farrell *et al.* (2004), *The Economist* (2005), Das (2006), Winters and Yusuf (2007), and Santos-Paulino and Wan (2010).

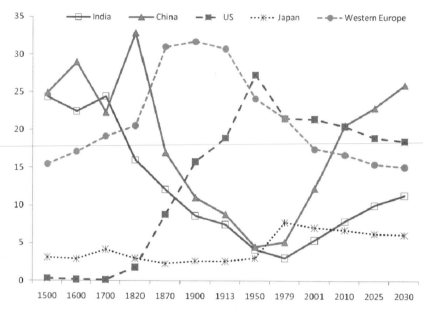

Figure 1.1 GDP Shares (%) of Selected Economies over the World Total, 1500–2030

Notes and sources: Data for 1500–2001 are based on Maddison (2003), who derived historical GDP figures in international dollars for the world economies. GDP shares for 2010, 2025 and 2030 are the author's own estimates by assuming average annual growth rates of 9.1% for China and 7.5% for India during 2001–2010, 5.6% for both countries during 2010–2030, 3% for the world economy during 2001–2030, and 2.5% for the US, Japan and Western Europe during 2001–2030. Western Europe includes Austria, Belgium, Denmark, Finland, France, Germany, Italy, the Netherlands, Norway, Sweden, Switzerland and the United Kingdom.

Since the initiative of economic reforms, China and India have enjoyed sustained economic growth for decades. Today the two countries together account for not only over one-third of the world's population, but also a substantial share of the world economy with China already being the world's second largest economy (in US dollar terms). Thus, understanding economic growth in these two developing giants has important implications for global economic and political affairs. This volume adds to the literature in the field and makes a timely contribution. This introductory chapter first presents a brief review of the literature comparing the economies of China and India (Section 1.1), and then outlines the issues to be discussed in the core chapters (Section 1.2).

1.1 Comparative Studies of the Chinese and Indian Economies

China and India have for a long time been popular comparators in the field of economic research.[2] Earlier studies comparing the economies of India and China focused on development in the 1950s and 1960s. Examples include Chen and Uppal (1971), Swamy (1973), Harris (1974) and Bergmann (1977). Recently, economists have again become interested in the comparison of the two giant developing economies largely due to their spectacular growth performance in the 1980s and 1990s, and subsequently their rising significance in the world economy and political affairs. Some authors are interested in the institutional setting and hence its impacts on economic performance in the two countries (Huang and Khanna, 2003). Others are keen to compare China's and India's performance in specific areas such as the steel industry (Etienne *et al.*, 1992), the grain marketing system (Zhou, 1997), the textile and clothing trade (Balasubramanyam and Wei, 2005a), electricity reforms (Xu, 2004), foreign direct investment (Negandhi and Schran, 1990; Balasubramanyam and Wei, 2005b; Sinha, 2007), the service sector (Wu, 2007), the energy sector (IEA, 2007), and technology and science (Baark and Sigurdson, 1981; Franda, 2002; McManus *et al.*, 2007).

There are also studies that deal with more general economic issues in the two countries. For example, Swamy (1989) and Das (2006) compare economic growth, Rosen (1992) contrasts models of industrial reforms, Bhalla (1995) discusses uneven development, Dzever and Jaussaud (1999) report on a series of studies of business strategies of firms, and Srinivasan (2004) sheds light on

---

[2] The literature review here is very brief. For more detailed coverage, the readers may refer to Swamy (1973), Das (2006), and Winters and Yusuf (2007).

macroeconomic performance. Several recent studies have focused on comparing the economic performance in China and India. Examples include Srinivasan (1994) on agriculture and trade, Kehal (2005) on foreign investment, Singh (2005) and Wu and Zhou (2006) on the bilateral economic relationship, Swamy (2003) and Srinivasan (2004) on reforms and economic performance, and Pandey and Dong (2009) on the role of institutional changes in manufacturing productivity.[3]

This book adds to the literature by focusing on economic growth and several growth-related issues, including growth at various levels (aggregate, regional and sectoral), trade, environmental pollution, energy consumption and carbon emissions. The analyses in this book are based on the latest data from both China and India. Considerable efforts have been made to reconcile the data so that the comparative analyses are based on consistent statistics of the two economies, which are managed in very different institutional settings. The core chapters are outlined in the next section.

1.2 Outline of the Chapters

The six core chapters (Chapters 2 to 7) of this book in turn deal with aggregate growth, regional growth, the service sector, international trade, energy and emissions, and environmental pollution in the two countries, as summarized in Table 1.1. Chapter 2 compares aggregate growth in China and India. It adds to the literature by examining and comparing several issues associated with economic growth in the two nations. In particular, it attempts to investigate the contributions of factor inputs and productivity to economic growth as well as discuss the growth prospects in the two countries. The role of productivity in economic growth has

---

[3] Other comparative studies include Hsieh and Klenow (2009) on factor misallocation and its impact on manufacturing productivity, Piketty and Qian (2009) on income tax reforms, Dougherty and Valli (2009) and Wan and Santos-Paulino (2008) who introduce two journal special issues, and Holslag (2010) on the Sino–Indian relationship.

Table 1.1 Summary Information of the Core Chapters

Chapters	Topics	Methods
2	Aggregate growth	Growth accounting
3	Regional growth	Regression analysis
4	Service sector growth	Determinants of services
5	Trade	Index approach
6	Energy/Emissions	Cross-country comparison
7	Pollution and growth	Descriptive analysis

Source: Author's own compilation.

implications for the possibility of sustained, high growth in China and India in the coming decades. In terms of growth prospects, this chapter will also explore growth potential at the sector level in the two economies.

Chapter 3 compares regional growth, disparity and convergence in the two economies. It presents a detailed examination of economic growth in the Chinese and Indian regions over the past 20 years. It also provides an assessment of regional disparity in the two countries, and investigates whether there is any evidence of regional convergence during the period of rapid economic growth. It attempts to identify the sources of regional disparity and hence draw policy implications for economic development in the two countries in the near future.

Over the decades of economic development, services in these two Asian giants have played a very different role. In India, the service sector contributes almost 60% of GDP, while its GDP share in China is much smaller (about 41% in 2009). To provide an explanation for the contrasting trajectories, Chapter 4 examines and compares service sector developments in these two Asian giants. More specifically, it investigates the determinants of demand for services and sheds light on the outlook for service sector growth in the two countries.

Bilateral trade between China and India, the world's two most populous countries, has expanded substantially in recent years. However, few studies have focused on the understanding of this trade relationship. Chapter 5 attempts to fill this void in the literature. Its objective is to examine and compare international trade in and between the two economies. In particular, this chapter investigates the major trends of and changes in the bilateral trade between the two countries, and explores issues associated with trade intensity, intra-industry trade and comparative advantages in the two countries. The findings are used to draw policy implications for future trade and economic cooperation between the two Asian developing giants.

The rise of China and India has important implications for the rest of the world. One area which has been intensely debated is energy consumption and the resultant consequences. These two nations are emerging not only as key players in the global energy market, but also as the main carbon emitters in the world due to their large volume of energy consumption (with China already being the world's largest carbon emitter). Where do China and India stand internationally in terms of energy consumption and carbon emissions? What can they learn from the experience of other developed economies? These are some of the questions to be investigated in Chapter 6. Specifically, this chapter aims to compare energy intensity and CO_2 emissions and their changing patterns over time among the world economies. It will link energy intensity and CO_2 emissions with the stages of economic development (the concept of the environmental Kuznets curve), and thus employ the cross-country comparison results to gain insights into energy consumption and carbon emissions in China and India. Special attention will be paid to the comparison of consumption and emission patterns between the two giants and other Asian economies.

Chapter 7 extends the topic in the preceding chapter to present a comparative analysis of pollution in the two countries. It reviews the situation of pollution, in particular industrial pollution in the two countries. The chapter also discusses the issues of climate change, and considers China and India from an international perspective. It attempts to identify the sources of pollution in the two economies and, hence, explore the possible policy responses to pollution control and international commitments.

Chapter 2

Growth Since the 1980s

2.1 Introduction

There are quite a few studies comparing economic growth in China and India.[1] A main weakness in these studies is that the two economies are largely analyzed separately in the sense that, in a paper or book, there are always separate sections or chapters dealing with China and India, respectively.[2] Little effort has been made to consolidate and integrate the materials and statistics about the two economies and, hence, to conduct truly comparative investigations. The present chapter attempts to make a contribution in this direction. It adds to the growing literature by examining and comparing the sources of economic growth in China and India. The rest of the chapter first presents some stylized facts about economic reforms and growth in the two nations (Section 2.2). This is followed by a discussion on the sources of growth (Section 2.3). Further discussion and sensitivity analysis are described in Section 2.4. Subsequently, the chapter sheds some light on the growth outlook for China and India (Section 2.5). The final section (Section 2.6) summarizes the main findings.

---

[1] See the literature review in Section 1.1, Chapter 1.

[2] Swamy (2003) is to some extent an exception, attempting to combine Chinese and Indian materials and statistics in a comparative perspective.

2.2 Stylized Facts About Economic Reforms and Growth in China and India

Economic growth in China and India over the past five decades can be broadly divided into two periods, that is, from the 1950s to the 1970s and from the 1980s to the present. During the first three decades after the foundation of the People's Republic of China (PRC) in 1949 and the independence of the Republic of India in 1947, policy makers of both countries endeavored to choose an appropriate development model and ended with a mix of failures and successes. There is a huge literature focusing on the comparison of the earlier development experience in the two countries.[3] In general, economic development models in China and India during the 1950s, 1960s and 1970s were largely patterned on the Soviet command economic system (Table 2.1). Within this system, a high degree of self-sufficiency was pursued and consumer goods imports were banned. As a result, the economies suffered from low productive efficiency and a distorted pattern of industrialization coupled with poor product quality and technological backwardness. The collapse of the system in Eastern Europe in the 1990s was the best testament to these problems.

In addition, economic development in China was interrupted by several disastrous political campaigns such as the Great Leap Forward (1958–1960) and the Cultural Revolution (1966–1976). In India, conservative thinking also dominated domestic policymaking in the 1960s and 1970s. The consequence is that economic growth in both countries, particularly China, experienced severe ups and downs during the decades before 1980 (Figure 2.1).[4] The overall performance was not very impressive

---

[3] Examples include Chen and Uppal (1971), Swamy (1973), Harris (1974) and Bergmann (1977).

[4] China conducted a nation-wide economic survey in 2005. The survey results released in January 2006 show that China's GDP in 2004 was underreported by 16.8% (Zhu, 2005). The discrepancy was mainly due to underreporting of service sector economic activities. The Chinese government subsequently revised

Table 2.1 Chronicle of Selected Events in China and India

Era	China	India
1940s	Foundation of PRC (1949)	Independence (1947)
1950s	1953–1957: 1st Five-Year Plan (FYP) 1958–1960: Great Leap Forward Policy adjustment	1951–1956: 1st FYP 1956–1961: 2nd FYP
1960s	Centrally planned system (communization) 1961–1965: 2nd FYP 1966–1970: 3rd FYP 1966: Cultural Revolution (start)	Centrally planned system (or Licence Raj) 1961–1966: 3rd FYP Price stabilization Decentralization
1970s	1971–1975: 4th FYP 1976–1980: 5th FYP 1976: Cultural Revolution (end) Grassroots rural reforms	1969–1974: 4th FYP 1974–1979: 5th FYP Nationalization of banks Green Revolution
1980s	Deng Xiaoping in charge 1981–1985: 6th FYP 1986–1990: 7th FYP Gradualist reforms Joint ventures, SEZs, etc.	Rajiv Gandhi in office 1980–1985: 6th FYP 1985–1990: 7th FYP New economic policies EOUs, EPZs, etc.
1990s	1991–1995: 8th FYP 1996–2000: 9th FYP Open cities/Urban reforms Privatization Deepening reforms	1992–1997: 8th FYP 1997–2002: 9th FYP SEZs IMF-supported initiative abolishing Licence Raj
2000s	2001–2005: 10th FYP 2006–2010: 11th FYP 2001: WTO membership Global integration	2002–2007: 10th FYP 2007–2012: 11th FYP More liberalization Global integration

Notes and sources: Author's own compilation. EOUs, export oriented units; EPZs, export processing zones; SEZs, special economic zones; IMF, International Monetary Fund; WTO, World Trade Organization.

and released the country's historical GDP statistics back to 1993 (http://www.stats.gov.cn); official data pre-1993 were already updated in the past, according to economic survey results. Where possible, the newly released data are used throughout this book.

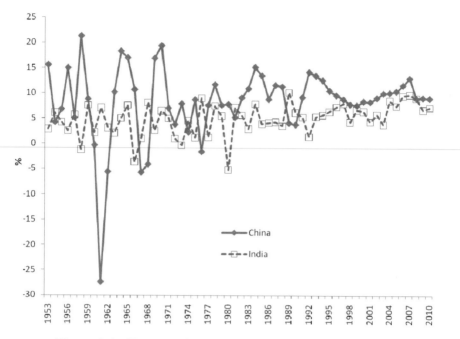

Figure 2.1   Economic Growth in China and India, 1953–2010

Notes and sources: Data are drawn from the NBS (2004, 2010) and RBI (2009). Chinese data are annual rates of growth. Indian data refer to growth rates in each financial year. Rates for 2010 are projected figures for India by the RBI (2010) and for China by the author.

in comparison with growth in other Asian economies during the same period. According to Table 2.2, during 1960–1980 per capita income doubled or tripled in most Asian economies, with the exception of China and India. The 1960s and 1970s were really the "lost" decades for these two economies.

Since the early 1980s, however, both China and India have moved away from the Soviet development model to more market-oriented systems.[5] This policy shift has spurred sustained, rapid growth in both countries over the past two decades, with an average annual rate of growth of 9.8% in China and 5.8% in India

---

[5] For surveys of economic reforms in China and India, see Reynolds (1987), Perkins (1988), Naughton (1996), Swamy (2003) and Mooij (2005).

Table 2.2   Growth Rates and Per Capita GDP in Selected Economies

	GDPpc (PPP\$, constant prices)		Average Growth Rates (%)	
	1960	**1980**	**1960s**	**1970s**
India	766	882 (260)	4.0	2.9
China	567	972 (305)	3.0	7.4
Indonesia	638	1,281 (645)	4.2	7.9
Korea	904	3,093 (1,646)	11.2*	7.7
Thailand	943	2,178 (696)	8.2	6.9
Philippines	1,133	1,879 (672)	4.9	5.9
Taiwan	1,256	4,459 (2,319)	9.3	9.8
Malaysia	1,420	3,799 (1,780)	6.5	7.9
Singapore	1,658	7,053 (4,904)	9.9	8.8
Japan	2,954	10,072 (9,120)	10.5	4.5

Notes and sources: Author's own estimates using data from the RBI (2004), NBS (1997), Easterly and Yu (2000), and IMF (2005). The numbers in parentheses are per capita GDP in US dollars. *This figure is based on the last four years of the 1960s.

during 1980–2010 (Figure 2.1). This growth in China (since 1980) and India (since 1991) has hit the news headlines because of its scale and impacts on the rest of the world. It has turned China into the "world factory" and increasingly the "world market", while India has become multinational companies' favorite destination for outsourcing. In particular, rapid growth in these two most populous nations has lifted tens of millions of people out of poverty.

Generally speaking, growth in China and India has been associated with domestic reforms, including economic liberalization as well as openness to trade and foreign investment. Chronologically, China started economic reforms a few years ahead of India. China's reforms began in the rural sector in the late 1970s, first through cautious experiments and then with widespread application of the household responsibility system (McMillan *et al.*, 1989; Lin, 1992). China's reforms in the urban sector and non-farming sectors took place in the mid-1980s. They were very slow and followed a gradualist approach. More comprehensive economic liberalization did not take place until the early 1990s. Indian reformers adopted a very similar approach towards economic liberalization, though the progress of reforms in the 1980s was even slower than China's. The initial reforms started following the election of Rajiv Gandhi as the Prime Minister in 1984, and went through several short episodes of liberalization (Mooij, 2005, p. 29).

There are similarities in the implementation of reforms in China and India. On the one hand, the reforms in China began in the form of "experiments" following the doctrine of the so-called "crossing the river by touching the stones". On the other hand, in India, "liberalization by stealth" was introduced under the guise of continuity (Panagariya, 2004, p. 5). Reforms were undertaken through isolated, sporadic liberalizing actions.[6] These reform approaches were adopted to avoid evoking serious political opposition in both countries. Reforms did not gain full momentum in India until the economic crisis in 1991, when a reform package supported by the International Monetary Fund (IMF) was put into practice; while in China full-scale reform was implemented only after 1992, when the then-Chinese leader Deng Xiaoping toured South China in the aftermath of the 1989 political crisis. The impact of these reforms on economic growth is clearly demonstrated in Figure 2.1. During the five years from 1992 to 1996, the average growth rate was 12.4% in China and 6.7% in India. Since then, a literature comparing various aspects of recent economic growth in the two countries has emerged.[7] This chapter adds to the existing literature by specifically examining the

---

[6] The impact of reforms on India's economic growth in the 1980s is still being debated (see Rodrik and Subramanian, 2005; Srinivasan, 2005).

[7] Examples include Zhou (1997) on the grain marketing system, Balasubramanyam and Wei (2005a) on the textile and clothing trade, Xu (2004) on electricity reforms, Negandhi and Schran (1990) and Balasubramanyam and Wei (2005b) on foreign direct investment, Bhalla (1995) on uneven development, Dzever and Jaussaud (1999) on business strategies of firms, and Srinivasan (2004) on macroeconomic performance.

sources of recent growth in the two countries, which is the topic of the next section.

2.3 Sources of Growth

The sources of growth can be examined following the conventional growth-accounting approach, which decomposes the rate of GDP growth into three components: the contributions of labor and capital inputs, and a residual or unexplained item. This technique is based on the following production function under the assumption of constant returns to scale:

$$Y = f(K, L, t), \qquad (2.1)$$

where Y, K, L and t represent output, capital and labor inputs, and time, respectively. Totally differentiating and dividing by Y both sides of Equation (2.1), one obtains

$$\dot{y} = \alpha_k \dot{k} + \alpha_l \dot{l} + T\dot{F}P, \qquad (2.2)$$

where the dot and α_i represent the percentage rate of growth and share of the ith factor input, respectively. With perfect competition, production factors are assumed to be paid their marginal products. The last item on the right-hand side of Equation (2.2) is defined as the rate of growth in total factor productivity (TFP), which is the difference between output growth and the factor-share-weighted rate of growth in factor inputs. It is also called the residual of output growth unexplained by input changes. Equation (2.2) thus implies that output growth is the sum of the weighted growth in factor inputs and total factor productivity growth.

The empirical application of Equation (2.2) is often complicated due to the lack of data on capital stock and factor shares for countries like China and India. The empirical analysis in this section begins with the estimation of capital stock series for China and India. While the governments of the two countries do not publish capital stock statistics, gross capital formation data are available from 1953 onwards. Given these datasets, the value of capital stock can be estimated following the conventional perpetual inventory approach. Symbolically, the estimation technique can be expressed as

$$K_t = (1 - \delta)K_{t-1} + \Delta K_t, \tag{2.3}$$

where K_t is the real value of capital stock in the tth year, ΔK_t is the real value of the incremental capital stock and δ is the rate of depreciation. Assuming that the initial capital stock in t_0 is K_{t_0}, Equation (2.3) can then be converted into

$$K_t = \sum_0^{t-t_0-1}(1-\delta)^j \Delta K_{t-j} + K_{t_0}(1-\delta)^{t-t_0}. \tag{2.4}$$

In Equation (2.4), the only unknowns are the initial value of capital stock (K_{t_0}) and the rate of depreciation (δ). In the existing literature, there are some estimates of the value of capital stock in 1952 as the initial year for China (e.g. Chow, 1993; Li *et al.*, 1995). Various rates of depreciation have also been used. Nehru and Dhareshwar (1993) present a cross-country capital stock database covering both China and India; however, these datasets are outdated and were derived under strong assumptions. In this chapter, to derive capital stock series for China and India, the available series of gross capital formation is back-casted to the year 1900 and it is assumed that the value of capital stock in 1900 was zero for both countries. This assumption is acceptable as any value recorded in 1900 would be worn out from 1980 onwards, namely, the period covered by this study. The choice of the rate of depreciation is largely based on China's aggregate and sectoral information.[8] After a series of rigorous tests, the rate of depreciation is assumed to be 4% for the period

---

[8] Indian data at the sector level are hardly available.

before 1980 and 4.5% from 1980 onwards.[9] Given these assumptions, the growth rates of the estimated capital stock together with the growth rates of GDP for the two countries are presented in Figure 2.2.[10]

Several conclusions can be drawn from Figure 2.2. First, capital accumulation has been growing much faster in China than in India since 1980. Second, in both countries, the rates of economic growth and capital accumulation have moved closely, reflecting the important role of capital input in boosting economic growth. Third, the figure implies that the difference in the rates of economic growth almost matches the variation in the rates of capital accumulation in the two countries. Therefore, it can be anticipated that capital input may be a major contributor to economic growth in both economies. Finally, in the last five years, the gap between China and India in terms of capital accumulation and growth has narrowed rapidly.

To apply Equation (2.2) for the growth accounting exercises, the remaining task is to estimate the factor shares. Due to data constraints, this chapter assumes constant returns to scale and hence focuses on the estimation of labor share in total factor payments; capital share is then the difference between unity and labor share. The Chinese government publishes detailed

---

[9] China's central government has published gross capital formation data for the period 1952–2004 and the value of depreciation for the period 1978–2004 for all Chinese regions. A simulation process was employed to derive the rate of depreciation so that the given values of depreciation are consistent with the assumed rates of depreciation for each region. It was found that there are regional variations in the rates of depreciation, which has never been addressed in the literature (Wu, 2008). It was also found that the rates of depreciation are generally lower in the poor regions than those in the relatively more developed regions. The rates are also slightly higher in the 1990s than in the 1980s. The GDP-weighted average rate of depreciation is about 4.5% in recent decades. Incidentally, this rate is close to the rate of 4% used by Nehru and Dhareshwar (1993) and the World Bank (1997).

[10] The derived capital stock series for both countries are reported in the Appendix to this chapter (Table A2.1).

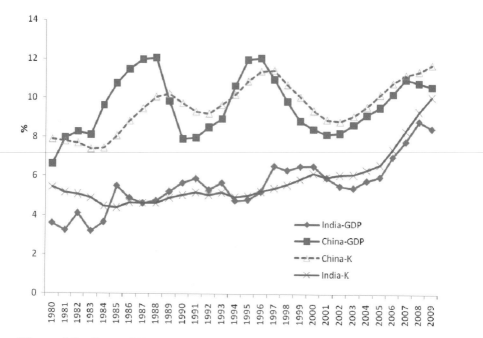

Figure 2.2   Rates of Economic Growth and Capital Accumulation, 1980–2009

Notes and sources: Author's own calculation. The rates are five-year moving averages of the rates of growth in GDP and capital stock in China and India, respectively.

information about employee compensation (including both salary and benefits-in-kind) for Chinese regions and the three economic sectors — the agricultural (or primary), manufacturing (or secondary) and services (or tertiary) sectors.[11] The estimated labor share is 0.53 for the 1980s (until 1991) and 0.52 for the period 1992–2009.[12] Thus, the corresponding shares for capital inputs are 0.47 for the period 1980–1991 and 0.48 for the period

---

[11] The manufacturing and services sectors are defined with slight differences in China and India. These are consolidated to a consistent system. As a result, the manufacturing sector is broadly defined to include the mining, manufacturing and construction industries. All other sectors fall into the services category.

[12] These shares are weighted averages among the Chinese regions.

Table 2.3   Sources of Economic Growth in China and India

	China				India			
	K	**L**	**TFP**	**Total**	**K**	**L**	**TFP**	**Total**
1980–1989	48.5	18.3	33.2	100	37.2	23.9	38.9	100
1990–1999	54.2	6.8	39.0	100	54.5	21.6	23.9	100
2000–2009	52.2	4.8	43.0	100	57.2	18.6	24.1	100
1980–2009	51.6	10.0	38.4	100	49.6	21.4	29.0	100

Notes and sources: Author's own calculation. The numbers are percentage shares calculated using raw data drawn from the NBS (2004, 2010), RBI (2009), Jha (2004), *Economic Survey 2004–2005* (2005), Planning Commission (2005) and Ministry of Labour and Employment (2010).

1992–2009. These shares are used for both China and India at this stage.[13] The results of the decomposition of the rates of growth are summarized in Table 2.3.

Table 2.3 demonstrates that, in contrast to the claims by Krugman (1994), Kim and Lau (1994) and Young (1994), total factor productivity growth has played an important role in economic growth in both China and India, accounting for about one-third of the rate of GDP growth on average. Table 2.3 also shows that capital input has been the dominant contributor to economic growth in both countries, with a slightly higher share in China reflecting the fact that China has invested much more than India. The latter has, however, caught up in the last decade. India also tends to gain relatively more from an increase in labor input than China. This is largely due to the expansion of the service sector in India. The share of the primary sector in the Indian economy is also relatively larger than that in the Chinese economy. Moreover, statistics show that

---

[13] Ideally, the analysis should be conducted at the sector level (agriculture, manufacturing and services). But, sectoral statistics in India are hardly available. For the purpose of comparison, this study focuses on the national level. For sector-oriented investigations of China as an individual country, the readers may refer to Fan *et al.* (2003) and Fan and Zhang (2002).

India's labor force is much younger than China's. Therefore, labor input will remain a nontrivial contributor to economic growth in India. This demographic advantage (or demographic dividends) that India holds over China will last for decades (Wilson and Purushothaman, 2003). However, in absolute terms, the contribution of labor input to economic growth has shown a declining trend in both countries. Thus, economic growth will rely on capital accumulation and technological progress (or productivity growth), especially the latter, in the long run.

2.4 Further Discussions

To extend the preceding discussion, this section has two objectives. The first objective is to conduct a sensitivity analysis of the empirical findings in Section 2.3. It investigates how the structural difference between the two economies affects the estimation results. The second objective is to briefly look at growth at the sector level.

2.4.1 *Sensitivity Analysis*

One may question the eligibility of applying the same factor shares and rates of depreciation for both countries. To gain some insight into this question, the structure of the two economies is examined first. Table 2.4 contrasts the structure of the Chinese and Indian economies (more detailed data are presented in the Appendix to this chapter in Table A2.2). The main difference between the two economies is the development of the manufacturing and service sectors. While the manufacturing sector is the dominant contributor to China's GDP, the service sector accounted for more than half of India's GDP in 2003. In addition, in terms of GDP shares, the role of the agricultural sector has been declining in both economies, though this sector is still the largest provider of jobs. Information at the sector level in China shows that the share of each factor over total factor payments varies considerably between

Table 2.4   Sector Shares (%) of GDP and Employment

	China			India		
	1983	**1995**	**2009**	**1983**	**1995**	**2009**
GDP shares						
Agriculture	36.3	19.2	9.2	36.4	29.5	17.0
Manufacturing	30.6	43.4	49.3	22.5	23.3	23.8
Services	33.1	37.4	41.6	41.1	47.1	59.3
Employment shares						
Agriculture	67.1	52.2	38.3	63.2	59.3	52.0
Manufacturing	18.7	23.0	27.7	15.3	16.0	14.0
Services	14.2	24.8	34.0	21.5	24.7	34.0

Notes and sources: GDP shares are based on 2000 (or 1999/2000 financial year) constant prices. All shares are the author's own calculation using data from the RBI (2009), Jha (2004), NBS (2010) and CIA (2010). The manufacturing sector includes mining, manufacturing and construction.

Table 2.5   Sources of India's Economic Growth: Alternative Results

Periods	K	L	TFP	Total
1980–1989	33.2	26.2	40.6	100
1990–1999	48.8	23.7	27.5	100
2000–2009	51.3	20.4	28.3	100
1980–2009	44.4	23.4	32.1	100

Notes and sources: Author's own calculation.

the sectors.[14] If these structural differences are taken into consideration, one can derive a slightly greater labor share for India, that is, 0.58 for the 1980s and 0.57 for the more recent decade. The re-estimated results using these shares show some minor variations in the sources of growth which, however, do not alter the conclusions drawn in the preceding section (Table 2.5).

---

[14] It was found that the share of labor input among total factor payments was 86% for the agricultural sector, 38% for the manufacturing sector and 46% for the service sector during 1978–2002.

Table 2.6   Summary of Findings in the Literature

Authors	Period	K	L	TFP	δ	α_l
Indian economy						
This study	1980–2004	47	20	33	4.5	52
Swamy (2003)	1980–1997	52	15	33	n.a.	n.a.
Guha-Khasnobis and Bari (2003)	1980s	30	34	36	4.0	67
Guha-Khasnobis and Bari (2003)	1990s	29	24	47	4.0	67
Chinese economy						
This study	1980–2004	50	11	39	4.5	52
Maddison (1998)	1978–1995	49	21	30	n.a.	60
Chow and Li (2002)	1978–1998	55	13	32	5.4	44
Swamy (2003)	1980–1997	39	16	45	n.a.	n.a.
Hu and Khan (1997)	1979–1994	46	13	41	3.6	45
World Bank (1997)	1978–1995	37	17	46	4.0	60
Bosworth and Collins (2003)	1980–1990	23	31	46	5.0	65
Bosworth and Collins (2003)	1990–2000	32	18	50	5.0	65

Notes and sources: Statistics in this table are the author's own compilation from the studies cited. Modifications where applicable were made so that the statistics are compatible. The numbers in the δ column are the rates of depreciation used, and those in the α_l column are the labor shares employed.

There is a large literature that applies the growth-accounting approach to investigate the source of recent growth in China, while few studies have focused on India. The conclusions drawn so far can also be compared with the findings in the existing literature, which are summarized in Table 2.6. In general, it is found that TFP growth has played a significant role in economic growth in both China and India during the last few decades. This provides the foundation for sustainable growth in the long run. However, capital accumulation is found to be the largest contributor to economic growth. Thus, high growth in both nations has been supported by high investment.

2.4.2 *Growth at the Sector Level*

At the sectoral level, in accordance with the finding by Kuznets (1971), the role of agriculture in both economies has been declining

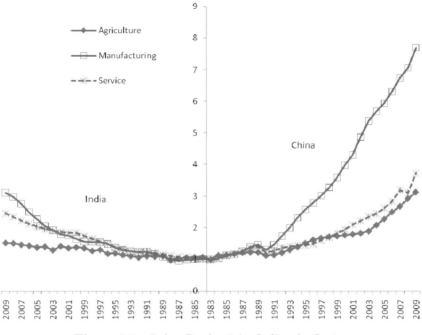

Figure 2.3   Labor Productivity Indices by Sector

Notes and sources: Labor productivity indices are relative to the 1983 level which is set at 1, and based on 2000 (or 1999/2000 financial year) constant prices.

over time (Table 2.4). Apart from this, however, China and India have pursued very different development models at the sector level. China's manufacturing sector has become the major contributor of economic growth, driven largely by rapidly increasing labor productivity (Figure 2.3). Meanwhile, the service sector has been the main driving force behind India's economic growth, though no exceptional labor productivity growth has been recorded. Growth was more balanced in the 1980s in both countries; but since the early 1990s, growth in the two economies has been very unbalanced at the sector level. In China, growth in the service sector is lagging behind the manufacturing sector. In contrast, India's service sector has outpaced other sectors to become the main contributor to GDP growth (Table 2.7).

Table 2.7 Contributions to Growth at the Sector Level

Periods	China			India		
	A	**M**	**S**	**A**	**M**	**S**
1980–1989	18.9	34.7	46.5	28.8	22.6	48.6
1990–1999	8.0	53.6	38.4	16.7	23.1	60.2
2000–2009	5.0	51.6	43.4	7.7	24.9	67.4

Notes and sources: A, M and S represent the agricultural, manufacturing and service sectors, respectively. The numbers are percentage shares over the incremental GDP between the starting and ending years in each period, and based on the author's own calculation. Raw data are based on 2000 (or 1999/2000 financial year) constant prices and drawn from the RBI (2009) and NBS (2004, 2010).

2.5 Growth Outlook

Historical experiences show that, during the process of economic development, countries in the world have followed the pattern of ladder-climbing with those on the top losing their comparative advantage in labor-intensive manufacturing to the climber below.[15] For example, in East Asia, Japan gradually lost its comparative advantage in labor-intensive manufacturing to the four East Asian tiger economies in the 1960s and 1970s, who in turn lost it to China and India in the 1980s and 1990s.[16] Each shift in comparative advantage takes about 20 to 30 years. For subcontinental economies like China and India, they can exploit their own internal ladder-climbing development model due to the existence of regional disparity. The latter is clearly demonstrated in Figure 2.4. Some regional economies, such as the coastal areas in China as well as Gujarat, Maharashtra and Chandigarh in India, have outperformed others and hence are on the top of the ladder. The less developed regions will eventually catch up with the more

---

[15] Some authors have also explored this issue in terms of the flying geese theory (Korhonen, 1994) and the product cycle model (Hill and Fujita, 1995).

[16] The four tiger economies refer to South Korea, Taiwan, Hong Kong and Singapore.

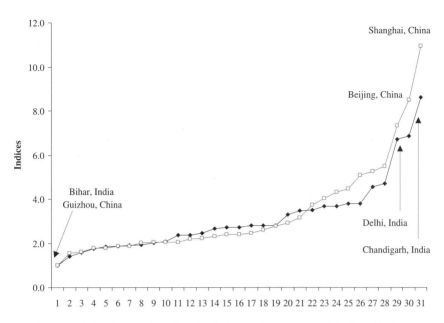

Figure 2.4   Income Per Capita Indices of Chinese and Indian States

Notes and sources: The states in each country are ranked according to their income per capita in 2007. The indices are per capita income relative to the poorest state in each country (Guizhou in China and Bihar in India). The raw data are based on 1999/2000 constant prices. Nagaland of India is excluded due to missing data.

developed areas.[17] Thus, China and India can maintain their comparative advantages in labor-intensive manufacturing for a lot longer (e.g. 50 years) than other economies such as the four Asian Tigers.

Through international comparisons, Kuznets (1971) concluded that a high rate of growth is for the most part attributable to a high rate of productivity growth. As shown in the preceding section, economic growth in both China and India has partly been driven by TFP growth, implying a sound foundation and thus an optimistic outlook for growth in the two countries. This

---

[17] Problems associated with regional disparity are not discussed here. Readers may refer to Jian *et al.* (1996) and Renard (2002) on China, and Kalirajan and Sankar (2003) and Jha (2005) on India.

positive aspect is further strengthened by the high (in China) and rising (in India) rate of investment in the two economies. These two factors, i.e. TFP growth and high rate of capital accumulation, determine that China and India will maintain the current rate of growth for at least another two decades. These two factors were also found to be vital for the growth of the American economy during 1960–1989 (Dougherty and Jorgenson, 1996).

At the sector level, China's service sector development is lagging behind from an international perspective (Figure 2.5). Thus, strong growth is anticipated in China's service sector. India, however, appears to be close to the world average according to Figure 2.5. But, among the less developed economies, India is one of the outliers whose service sector has outpaced economic development at the national level. For example, if one focuses on economies with a per capita income of less than PPP$10,000, a visual examination of Figure 2.5 can reveal that India is well above the average.

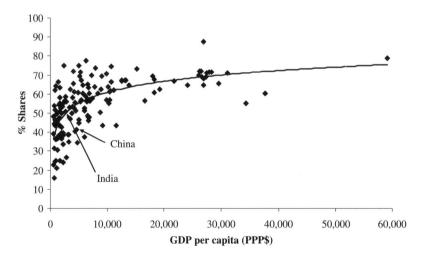

Figure 2.5   Service Sector Shares over GDP vs. GDP Per Capita, 2003

Notes and sources: GDP per capita at purchasing power parity is drawn from the IMF (2005). GDP shares of the service sectors are extracted from the World Bank (2005). Countries with missing data are excluded from both databases.

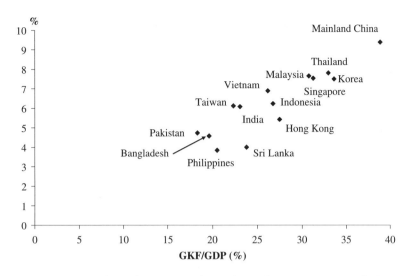

Figure 2.6   Growth Rates vs. Gross Capital Formation over GDP

Notes and sources: The *Y*-axis and *X*-axis represent average GDP growth rates and ratios of gross capital formation (GKF) over GDP, respectively, during the period 1987–2004 (1997 and 1998 are excluded). The numbers are calculated using data from the ADB (2005).

In terms of the ratio of investment over GDP, India and two other South Asian economies, Pakistan and Bangladesh, are at the low tail of the scattered chart in Figure 2.6. Among the small samples presented in Figure 2.6, it seems that India has achieved more than what the country invests. Given this reality, India's economic performance is above the average. However, in comparison with East Asian economies, India is far short of investment. Thus, to catch up with China, India would have to save and invest a lot more in the near future. For example, if India's capital stock could grow at the same rate as China's, this would add another 1.6 percentage points to India's rate of economic growth.[18] In addition, another area that would boost Indian investment is the inflow of foreign direct investment (FDI). In comparison with China's FDI of US$54 billion in 2003, India's FDI of US$5 billion in the same year was too little.[19]

---

[18] Calculated by assuming a rate of depreciation of 4% and capital share of 40%.

[19] According to the NBS (2004) and RBI (2004).

There is definitely potential for India to get its policies right and attract more foreign investment.

2.6 Conclusion

Economic reforms and the resultant rapid growth in China and India have triggered a growing interest in comparing the economic performance of these two Asian giants. This chapter adds to the literature by first consolidating statistics of the two countries and then investigating several issues associated with growth. It is found that recent growth in China and India has been driven by productivity growth and fast accumulation of capital stock. A substantial contribution of TFP implies the possibility of sustained high growth in the two economies in the coming decades. In particular, there is considerable growth potential in China's service sector and India's manufacturing sector.

As agriculture declines in the economies, rural out-migrants will have to be absorbed by the expansion of the service sector. This is especially so in China, where the job-creation capacity of the manufacturing sector is very much saturated and future growth in employment lies largely in the service sector. In India, the dilemma is that the service sector is the largest contributor of GDP but relatively few jobs are created in this sector. To absorb rural surplus labor, India needs a manufacturing boom similar to the one which took off a decade ago in China. In addition, India has not achieved the same level of growth as China has largely because of the difference in the rate of investment growth. There is great scope for more investment, both domestic and foreign, in India. However, in terms of capital utilization, India appears to be more efficient than China. Therefore, while the two countries' experience offers lessons to other transitional and developing economies, China and India can also learn from each other.

Appendix

Table A2.1 Capital Stock Series for China and India

Year	China (billion yuan)	India (billion rupee)	China (index)	India (index)
1950	376	2,732	100	100
1951	410	2,982	109	109
1952	448	3,171	119	116
1953	507	3,304	135	121
1954	575	3,424	153	125
1955	639	3,598	170	132
1956	716	3,841	190	141
1957	800	4,158	213	152
1958	941	4,473	250	164
1959	1,149	4,736	305	173
1960	1,326	5,024	353	184
1961	1,366	5,366	363	196
1962	1,371	5,735	365	210
1963	1,409	6,132	375	224
1964	1,474	6,593	392	241
1965	1,575	7,102	419	260
1966	1,712	7,612	455	279
1967	1,792	8,144	477	298
1968	1,869	8,681	497	318
1969	1,969	9,182	524	336
1970	2,164	9,731	575	356
1971	2,376	10,273	632	376
1972	2,570	10,870	684	398
1973	2,797	11,449	744	419
1974	3,026	12,070	805	442
1975	3,296	12,694	877	465
1976	3,530	13,354	939	489
1977	3,790	14,082	1,008	515
1978	4,134	14,850	1,100	544
1979	4,484	15,766	1,192	577
1980	4,818	16,540	1,281	605
1981	5,135	17,190	1,366	629
1982	5,490	18,055	1,460	661
1983	5,905	18,869	1,571	691

(Continued)

Table A2.1 *(Continued)*

Year	China (billion yuan)	India (billion rupee)	China (index)	India (index)
1984	6,418	19,635	1,707	719
1985	7,102	20,537	1,889	752
1986	7,842	21,598	2,086	791
1987	8,630	22,654	2,295	829
1988	9,543	23,677	2,538	867
1989	10,441	24,970	2,777	914
1990	11,302	26,287	3,006	962
1991	12,245	27,811	3,257	1,018
1992	13,413	29,010	3,567	1,062
1993	15,137	30,486	4,026	1,116
1994	16,954	31,816	4,509	1,165
1995	18,940	33,601	5,037	1,230
1996	21,008	35,911	5,587	1,314
1997	23,057	37,742	6,132	1,381
1998	25,175	40,012	6,695	1,465
1999	27,405	42,289	7,289	1,548
2000	29,656	45,326	7,887	1,659
2001	32,219	47,995	8,569	1,757
2002	35,208	50,721	9,364	1,857
2003	38,937	53,857	10,355	1,971
2004	43,327	57,549	11,523	2,106
2005	48,236	62,437	12,829	2,285
2006	53,847	68,603	14,321	2,511
2007	59,945	75,736	15,943	2,772
2008	66,821	84,141	17,772	3,080
2009	75,478	93,077	20,074	3,407

Notes and sources: The data are based on the author's own estimates and expressed in 2000 (or 1999/2000) constant prices.

Table A2.2 GDP and Employment Shares (%) by Sector in China and India

	GDP			Employment		
	Agriculture	Manufacturing	Services	Agriculture	Manufacturing	Services
India						
1982–83	36.4	22.5	41.1	63.2	15.3	21.5
1983–84	37.1	22.6	40.3	62.5	15.7	21.8
1984–85	36.3	22.5	41.2	61.9	16.1	22.0
1985–86	35.0	22.5	42.5	61.2	16.5	22.3
1986–87	33.4	22.7	43.9	60.1	17.2	22.6
1987–88	31.7	23.1	45.1	60.2	16.9	22.9
1988–89	33.3	22.9	43.8	60.3	16.6	23.2
1989–90	31.8	23.3	44.9	60.3	16.3	23.4
1990–91	31.4	23.7	44.9	60.3	16.0	23.7
1991–92	30.3	23.3	46.4	60.4	15.7	24.0
1992–93	30.7	22.7	46.6	60.4	15.4	24.2
1993–94	30.0	22.7	47.3	59.8	15.7	24.5
1994–95	29.5	23.3	47.1	59.3	16.0	24.7
1995–96	27.3	24.4	48.3	58.7	16.3	25.0
1996–97	27.8	24.1	48.1	58.0	16.6	25.4
1997–98	26.0	23.9	50.1	57.4	16.9	25.7
1998–99	25.9	23.3	50.8	56.7	17.2	26.1
1999–2000	25.0	22.8	52.2	56.2	16.9	26.8
2000–01	23.9	23.4	52.7	55.7	16.5	27.5

(Continued)

Table A2.2   (Continued)

	GDP			Employment		
	Agriculture	Manufacturing	Services	Agriculture	Manufacturing	Services
2001–02	24.0	22.7	53.3	55.2	16.2	28.2
2002–03	21.4	23.5	55.1	54.8	15.9	29.0
2003–04	21.7	23.3	55.0	54.3	15.5	29.8
2004–05	20.2	23.9	55.8	53.8	15.2	30.6
2005–06	19.5	24.2	56.3	53.4	14.9	31.4
2006–07	18.5	24.6	56.9	52.9	14.6	32.2
2007–08	17.8	24.4	57.8	52.5	14.3	33.1
2008–09	17.0	23.8	59.3	52.0	14.0	34.0
China						
1983	36.3	30.6	33.1	67.1	18.7	14.2
1984	35.5	30.3	34.2	64.0	19.9	16.1
1985	32.1	31.9	35.9	62.4	20.8	16.8
1986	30.5	32.4	37.1	60.9	21.9	17.2
1987	28.8	33.1	38.1	60.0	22.2	17.8
1988	26.7	34.3	39.0	59.4	22.4	18.3
1989	26.4	34.2	39.4	60.0	21.6	18.3
1990	27.2	33.9	38.8	60.1	21.4	18.5
1991	25.6	35.5	38.9	59.7	21.4	18.9
1992	23.6	37.9	38.5	58.5	21.7	19.8

(Continued)

Table A2.2 (*Continued*)

	GDP			Employment		
	Agriculture	Manufacturing	Services	Agriculture	Manufacturing	Services
1993	21.8	40.1	38.1	56.4	22.4	21.2
1994	20.2	42.2	37.6	54.3	22.7	23.0
1995	19.2	43.4	37.4	52.2	23.0	24.8
1996	18.4	44.4	37.3	50.5	23.5	26.0
1997	17.4	44.8	37.8	49.9	23.7	26.4
1998	16.7	45.3	38.0	49.8	23.5	26.7
1999	16.0	45.5	38.6	50.1	23.0	26.9
2000	15.1	45.9	39.0	50.0	22.5	27.5
2001	14.3	46.0	39.7	50.0	22.3	27.7
2002	13.5	46.3	40.2	50.0	21.4	28.6
2003	12.6	47.4	40.0	49.1	21.6	29.3
2004	12.1	47.8	40.0	46.9	22.5	30.6
2005	11.6	48.4	40.0	44.8	23.8	31.3
2006	10.9	48.9	40.2	42.6	25.2	32.2
2007	10.0	49.6	40.4	40.8	26.8	32.4
2008	10.2	51.0	38.9	39.6	27.2	33.2
2009	9.2	49.3	41.6	38.3	27.7	34.0

Notes and sources: GDP shares are based on 2000 (or 1999/2000 financial year) constant prices. All shares are the author's own calculation using data from the RBI (2009), Jha (2004), NBS (2010) and CIA (2010). The manufacturing sector includes mining, manufacturing and construction.

Chapter 3

Regional Growth and Convergence

This chapter adds to the preceding chapter by focusing on regional growth in the two countries. In particular, it attempts to explore how regional economies in the two vast countries have performed during the period of high growth, and assess whether regional disparity has deteriorated or not as economic liberalization deepens. It is found that substantial regional disparity exists in China and India. This disparity has shown an increasing trend in both countries during the period of rapid economic growth, especially since the early 1990s. However, the increase in regional disparity in both countries largely reflects the enlarging gap between the super-rich regions and the rest of the economy within each country. In other words, economic growth has not led to catch-up effects in the relatively poor regions as postulated by the new growth theories (Abramovitz, 1986). This study also shows that variations in infrastructure development and the level of urbanization are the main sources of regional disparity in both countries. In China, the export sector also plays a role in affecting regional development. In India, human capital development in recent years may also affect regional disparity.

The rest of this chapter is organized as follows. The next section (Section 3.1) presents some stylized facts about regional growth in the two economies. The chapter then sheds some light on regional convergence and divergence in the past few decades (Section 3.2). This is followed by regression analyses to explain the sources of regional disparity in Section 3.3. Concluding comments are presented in the final section (Section 3.4).

3.1 Regional Growth in China and India

During 1980–2009, China and India achieved phenomenal economic growth at an average rate of 9.8% and 5.8%, respectively.[1] These growth rates are unprecedented in the two countries' histories. However, there are substantial variations in growth across the regions of the two economies. Figure 3.1 presents the distribution of real gross regional product (GRP) per capita and GRP growth rates in China in 2007 and in India during the 2006/2007 financial year. Several observations can be made. First, in both countries, the regions (China's provinces and special municipalities as well as India's states and union territories) can be divided into two groups: the most

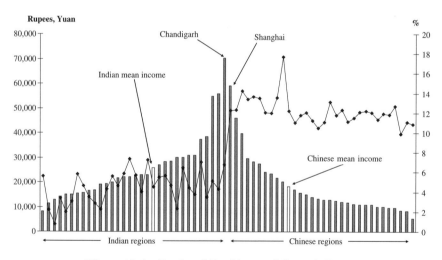

Figure 3.1 Regional Ranking and Growth Rates

Notes: Ranking is based on the value of 2007 gross provincial product (GPP) per capita in China and 2006/2007 financial year net state domestic product (NSDP) per capita in India. Growth rates are the average rates during 2001–2007. In 2007, US$1=40.8 rupees and 7.6 yuan. Data are drawn from the NBS (various issues) and RBI (2009).

---

[1] These rates are the author's own estimates, using official statistics of China and India published by the NBS (various issues) and RBI (2009), respectively.

urbanized areas, including Shanghai, Beijing and Tianjin in China and Chandigarh, Goa and Delhi in India; and the rest of the economies.[2] As expected, the most urbanized regions have the highest per capita income in both economies. Thus, one could conclude that the level of urbanization is positively associated with the level of economic development among the regions.

Second, the gap between the rich and the poor is much bigger in China than in India. For instance, the ratio of per capita GRP in China's richest region (Shanghai) over that in the country's poorest region (Guizhou) in 2007 was 10.9, which is much greater than the corresponding ratio of 8.6 in India (i.e. the ratio of per capita GRP in Chandigarh, the richest region, over that in Bihar, the poorest region). Third, if the super-rich regions (three municipalities and Zhejiang in China as well as four states in India) are excluded, regional disparity appears less severe in the two countries. Without the super-rich, the income ratio of the richest region over the poorest region was 5.5 in China and 4.7 in India in 2007. These ratios are still high but seem to be close to those in economies at a similar stage of development. For example, the per capita income ratio of the richest state over the poorest state was 5.8 in the US in 1900, 3.0 in Italy in 1950, 2.4 in France in 1950, 2.8 in Japan in 1955 and 2.2 in the US in 1990.[3]

As for the rates of regional growth, they are very diverse in both countries. According to Figure 3.1, as expected, the average rate of growth is much higher in China than in India. It seems that growth in China's more developed regions slowed down during 2001–2007 with the exception of Inner Mongolia, which had the highest average rate of growth. In India, the fastest-growing regions appear to be the "middle classes", i.e. those states with

---

[2] See Table A3.1 in the Appendix to this chapter for more details about urbanization in each region.

[3] These statistics are based on data reported in Barro and Sala-i-Martin (1995). Tokyo is excluded from the comparison.

per capita income ranked between the super-rich and the poorest states.

Perhaps due to these variations in the rates of growth, the ranking of the regions changed very differently in the two countries according to Table 3.1. In China, major changes occurred in the 1980s. Between 1980 and 1994, four of the top eight regions changed. The main winners in China were the coastal regions such as Zhejiang, Guangdong, Jiangsu, Fujian and Shandong. These regions were also the beneficiaries of China's economic reforms, as they were offered special policy initiatives under the concept of "letting some get rich first". Thus, economic policies have played an important role in affecting regional disparity in China in the past two decades. Since the 1990s, the same regions have occupied the top-eight group with minor changes in ranking among themselves. In India, the top eight members have been occupied by the same regions for over 25 years. In both countries, however, the bottom eight positions have been occupied by almost the same regions for more than two decades. Thus, the poor remain poor in both countries.

Therefore, with regard to changes in regional disparity over the past two decades, China and India are very different but they also share some similarities. One may argue that India's democratic system makes it difficult for the country to pursue an unbalanced development strategy as adopted by China during this period. The increasing regional disparity in China is hence partly attributed to the country's economic policies, while in India it may be more related to non-institutional factors such as historical and geographic reasons. For example, Rao *et al.* (1999) argue that India's more developed regions with relatively better infrastructure, human resources and accessibility to markets have been able to exploit the opportunities offered by economic liberalization better than the relatively poor states. Sachs *et al.* (2002) claim that Orissa's vulnerability to floods and devastation from tropical cyclones is partly attributable for its poor performance in agriculture and hence the overall economic conditions in the state.

Table 3.1 Ranking of Chinese and Indian Regional Economies

Chinese Regions	1981	1994	2007	Indian Regions	1981	1994	2006
Shanghai	1	1	1	Chandigarh	1	1	1
Beijing	2	2	2	Goa	3	3	2
Tianjin	3	3	3	Delhi	2	2	3
Zhejiang	12	5	4	Pondicherry	4	9	4
Guangdong	15	4	5	Haryana	8	7	5
Jiangsu	11	7	6	Maharashtra	7	6	6
Liaoning	4	6	7	Andaman and Nicobar Islands	6	4	7
Fujian	19	8	8	Punjab	5	5	8
Shandong	17	9	9	Himachal Pradesh	12	15	9
Inner Mongolia	13	15	10	Kerala	16	14	10
Heilongjiang	5	10	11	Tamil Nadu	17	11	11
Hebei	8	13	12	Gujarat	9	8	12
Jilin	9	12	13	Karnataka	15	16	13
Hubei	20	14	14	Tripura	24	25	14
Xinjiang	14	11	15	Andhra Pradesh	19	17	15
Shanxi	10	17	16	Sikkim	13	13	16
Henan	25	24	17	West Bengal	11	19	17
Hunan	21	19	18	Meghalaya	21	18	18
Ningxia	6	20	19	Nagaland	20	10	19
Qinghai	7	16	20	Arunachal Pradesh	14	12	20
Shaanxi	16	26	21	Jammu and Kashmir	10	21	21
Sichuan	24	22	22	Rajasthan	27	22	22
Anhui	27	21	23	Manipur	18	23	23
Jiangxi	23	25	24	Assam	25	24	24
Guangxi	22	18	25	Orissa	23	27	25
Yunnan	26	23	26	Madhya Pradesh	22	20	26
Gansu	18	27	27	Uttar Pradesh	26	26	27
Guizhou	28	28	28	Bihar	28	28	28

Notes: Ranking is based on the values of gross regional product (GRP) per capita in each (financial) year. Regions with missing values are dropped.

3.2 Regional Convergence or Divergence

In the growth literature, two types of convergence have been defined and applied: the σ-convergence and β-convergence (Barro and Sala-i-Martin, 1995). In this chapter, σ-convergence is measured by the coefficients of variation (CVs) of the gross regional product (GRP) per capita.[4] Two sets of samples are employed for each country. That is, one set contains all regions in each country and the other excludes the super-rich regions according to the 2007 ranking of per capita GRP. The estimation results are presented in Figure 3.2.

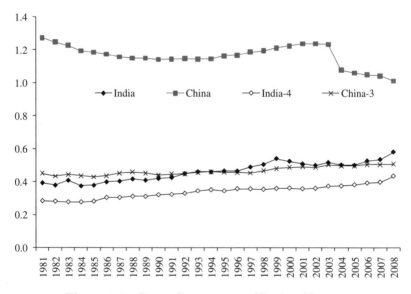

Figure 3.2 Sigma-Convergence of Regional Income

Notes: The Y-axis indicates the magnitude of the coefficients of variation of gross provincial product (GPP) per capita in China and net state domestic product (NSDP) per capita in India. India-4 is calculated excluding the four super-rich regions (Chandigarh, Goa, Delhi and Pondicherry), and China-3 is based on all regions but the three super-rich (Shanghai, Beijing and Tianjin).

---

[4] For the raw data, see Tables A3.2 and A3.3 in the Appendix to this chapter.

In comparison, Chinese regions show greater income dispersion than Indian regions according to Figure 3.2, which depicts the two curves for China above the Indian ones. In particular, there is a huge income gap between the three cities and the rest of China, though there is some evidence of convergence in recent years. The chart also presents evidence of modest regional convergence in China in the 1980s. This observation is consistent with findings reported in other studies (e.g. Raiser, 1998; Démurger *et al.*, 2002; Wu, 2004). However, since the early 1990s, Chinese regions have shown a tendency of divergence, which is mainly reflected in the widening gap between the three large municipalities and other provinces. Figure 3.2 clearly shows that the CVs across Chinese regions excluding the three municipalities hardly changed in the entire sample period, implying relatively stable income differences.

In the case of India, there is also an income gap between the super-rich and the rest of the country, as the CV values for the two groups are different. There was little change in regional disparity in the first half of the 1980s, but regional divergence has taken place modestly since 1984 when Rajiv Gandhi took office and initiated the first wave of economic reforms. However, the trend of regional divergence seems to have originated from different sources over time. In the late 1980s and early 1990s, divergence occurred mainly between regions excluding the four super-rich states (Chandigarh, Goa, Delhi and Pondicherry). This is clearly demonstrated in Figure 3.2, where the two curves for India are almost parallel to each other during that period though they show a rising trend. But since the late 1990s, when more comprehensive reforms were introduced, regional divergence seems to be driven both by the widening gap between the super-rich states and the rest of the economy and by modest divergence among the states. This is demonstrated by the modest rising trend of the two Indian CV curves and the slightly widening space between the two curves.

Hence, in both countries there is an income gap between the super-rich regions and other regions. This gap is much more serious in China than in India. However, it is increasing in India and has started falling modestly in China. In the absence of the super-rich, regional disparity showed only a minor increase during 1981–2008. This is in sharp contrast to popular perceptions about regional inequality in China and India during the reform periods (Jian *et al.*, 1996; Rao *et al.*, 1999).[5] Thus, in many existing studies, regional disparity may be inflated due to the impact of several highly urbanized economies among the regions (the three municipalities in China as well as Chandigarh, Goa and Delhi in India). To gain a better understanding of regional disparity, one should treat the super-rich regions separately.

The observed σ-convergence or divergence is mirrored in the estimation results of β-convergence, which are summarized in Table 3.2. The estimated values of β are derived from the following non-linear regression:

$$\log y_{iT} - \log y_{i0} = \alpha_0 + \alpha_1 \log y_{i0} + \varepsilon_i, \qquad (3.1)$$

Table 3.2   Estimation Results of Beta-Convergence: β Values

Periods	China	n	China-3	n
1981–1990	0.0027	29	−0.0059	26
1991–2000	0.0007	31	0.0023	28
1999–2008	0.0050	31	−0.0017	28
Periods	**India**	**n**	**India-4**	**n**
1980/1981–1989/1990	−0.0006	27	−0.0012	24
1990/1991–1999/2000	−0.0206	27	−0.0162	24
1998/1999–2007/2008	−0.0054	23	−0.0115	20

Notes: China-3 excludes Shanghai, Beijing and Tianjin; and India-4 does not include Chandigarh, Goa, Delhi and Pondicherry. The numbers under *n* represent the size of the samples used.

---

[5] In this study, "regional inequality" refers to inequality between provinces (and states) in China (and in India). Inequality within the provinces/states is not addressed here, but is becoming increasingly important in both countries. For empirical studies, see Knight *et al.* (2004) and Kanbur and Zhang (2005) on China, and Bhanumurthy and Mitra (2004) on India.

where y_{iT} and y_{i0} are income per capita at periods T and 0, respectively, ε_i is the standard white noise, and α_0 and α_1 are unknown parameters to be estimated with $\alpha_1 = -(1 - e^{-\beta T})$. A positive β-value indicates the existence of convergence. In the case of India, all scenarios considered here show evidence of regional divergence during 1981–2008. In China, the estimation results in Table 3.2 demonstrate a trend of regional convergence only if the three municipalities are included in the analysis. Thus, regional convergence reflects the catch-up effect in the first half of the 1980s; however, this implies a fall in the gap between the three largest cities (Shanghai, Beijing and Tianjin) and the rest of the country. Without the three municipalities, the findings in Table 3.2 do not show significant evidence of convergence among the regions in China.

To sum up, the results from the analyses of both sigma-convergence and beta-convergence illustrate that, during the period of high economic growth, the regions in China and India have shown a tendency of divergence. This has been mainly driven by the enlarging gap between several highly urbanized regions and the rest of the economy in the two countries. The trend of divergence seems to be relatively more severe in India than in China in recent years, though China's regional disparity in absolute terms is much worse than India's. In both countries, it seems that regional disparity has been relatively stable if several super-rich regions (provinces or states) are excluded from the analysis. This is contradictory to the popular perception that regional disparity has deteriorated significantly in both China and India since the early 1990s.

3.3 Sources of Regional Disparity: A Regression Analysis

The results discussed in the preceding sections indicate the existence of regional disparity in both China and India. There is, however, no evidence of regional convergence, though both economies have experienced phenomenal growth over the past few decades. This section attempts to provide an explanation of the sources of regional disparity. A regression approach is employed. To introduce this approach, consider the following income equation:

$$y = \beta_0 + \Sigma \beta_i x_i + \varepsilon, \tag{3.2}$$

where y represents a measure of income, e.g. income per capita, and x_i ($i = 1, ..., n$) are a list of variables that affect income. Equation (3.2) can be estimated using the ordinary least squares (OLS) technique. Given the estimates, $\hat{\beta}_i$, the prediction of income is $\hat{y} = \hat{\beta}_0 + \Sigma y^i = \hat{\beta}_0 + \Sigma \hat{\beta}_i x_i$. Morduch and Sicular (2002) show that the proportional contribution of the ith component to inequality measured using the variance or squared coefficient of variation is given as follows[6]:

$$S_{CV}^i = S_{Var}^i = \frac{\mathrm{cov}(y^i, y)}{\mathrm{var}(y)}. \tag{3.3}$$

To estimate the system of Equations (3.2) and (3.3), the following empirical model is considered:

$$\log(y) = f\,(inf,\ hum,\ urb,\ ind,\ z) + \varepsilon, \tag{3.4}$$

where y, *inf*, *hum*, *urb*, *ind* and z represent real gross regional product (GRP) per capita, infrastructure, human capital, urbanization, industrialization and a control variable, respectively. The selection of these variables and their definitions are very much dictated by the availability of regional data in the two countries. For the same reason, Equation (3.4) is estimated for each country using two one-year cross-sectional datasets representing the 1990s and the current period, respectively.[7] The variables identified in Equation (3.4) are also popular candidates in growth

---

[6] Recent applications of a similar technique include Zhang and Zhang (2003) and Wan (2004).

[7] The choice of one-single-year data is due to the unavailability of data in particular Indian regional statistics.

analyses.[8] A more detailed description of the variables is provided as follows.

Infrastructure. The condition of infrastructure development plays an important role in economic development. Well-developed infrastructure such as roads and telecommunications can help reduce business costs and improve efficiency, and hence is a key prerequisite for attracting domestic as well as foreign investment. The level of infrastructure development is expected to be positively related to income. For the India model, access to drinking water is employed as the proxy of infrastructure development and the information is available for each state for the years 1991 and 2001.[9] Another indicator that may also capture the activities of infrastructure development is investment in transport in each state.[10] This variable is included in the Indian model as a control variable. For the Chinese model, as access to drinking water is very much universal in China, telecommunication density across the regions is employed as a proxy of the level of infrastructure development.[11]

Human Capital. The role of human capital in economic growth is highlighted in the new growth theory (Benhabib and Spiegel, 1994). The measurement of human capital stock is, however, difficult and controversial.[12] This chapter simply employs regional literacy ratios as an indicator of the level of human capital development among the regions in China and India.

Urbanization. Preliminary analysis in the preceding section provides clear evidence about the relationship between the level of income and the degree of urbanization in both China and

---

[8] These variables are also included in the 60 variables identified by Sala-i-Martin (1997).

[9] The sources of data are listed in the Appendix to this chapter.

[10] Canning (1998) presents a detailed study of measuring the stock of infrastructure in the world.

[11] The same data for India are unfortunately not available.

[12] See, for example, Benhabib and Spiegel (1994), Pritchett (1997) and Temple (1998).

India. Thus, a variable reflecting the progress of urbanization is included in Equation (3.4) so that the contribution of urbanization to regional disparity is analyzed.

Industrialization. Regional disparity could be driven by structural differences between the regional economies in each country. More industrialized regions are expected to be more developed and consequently have a higher per capita income. For example, Bhattacharya and Sakthivel (2004) found that India's more industrialized states grew much faster than the less industrialized states during the reform period. To examine the effect of economic structure on regional disparity, the share of the manufacturing sector in GRP is employed as a proxy of the level of industrialization in the empirical models.

International trade. Openness to trade and investment is expected to play an important role in economic development.[13] This is confirmed by recent development experience in both China and India. The two economies, especially China, have benefited substantially from foreign investment and access to foreign markets through exports and imports. While regional trade figures are not available in India, the shares of the value of exports over GRP for the Chinese regions are included as a control variable.

The estimation results are presented in Table 3.3. The table shows that the chosen variables can explain a large proportion (70–90%) of the variation in regional income per capita. Another important conclusion that can also be drawn from the table is that variations in infrastructure development and urbanization are the main sources of regional disparity in both countries. This is consistent with the findings about the role of infrastructure by Nagaraj *et al.* (2000) and urbanization by Sachs *et al.* (2002). In addition, human resource development has played a key role in affecting regional disparity in recent years in India. In the case of China, international trade also plays a role in influencing regional

---

[13] There is a large body of literature on the relationship between economic development and trade. Readers may refer to Edwards (1992) and Harrison (1996).

Table 3.3 Estimation Results

Indian Model	1991		2001	
	$\hat{\beta}_i$	Shares (%)	$\hat{\beta}_i$	Shares (%)
Intercept	6.4987 (0.2258)*		6.8447 (0.3470)*	
Infrastructure	0.0067 (0.0027)**	24.5	0.0042 (0.0021)***	6.6
Human capital	0.0055 (0.0033)	8.1	0.0226 (0.0046)*	36.1
Urbanization	0.0086 (0.0034)**	25.5	0.0099 (0.0026)*	34.2
Industrialization	0.0058 (0.0070)	5.3	0.0099 (0.0040)**	8.5
Transport	9.8615 (2.7220)*	16.0	1.4260 (1.3281)	0.9
R^2	0.8064		0.8619	
Adjusted R^2	0.7554		0.8305	
Sample size	25		28	

Chinese Model	1990		2000	
	$\hat{\beta}_i$	Shares (%)	$\hat{\beta}_i$	Shares (%)
Intercept	6.7894 (0.2356)*		7.4887 (0.3377)*	
Infrastructure	0.0859 (0.0340)**	30.4	0.0480 (0.0117)*	65.7
Human capital	0.0013 (0.0036)	1.4	0.0370 (0.4396)	0.2
Urbanization	0.0139 (0.0045)*	37.2	0.0059 (0.0054)	15.7
Industrialization	0.0046 (0.0047)	6.7	0.0010 (0.0049)	0.5
Export	0.6489 (0.2497)**	11.9	0.4319 (0.3078)	9.2
R^2	0.8757		0.9129	
Adjusted R^2	0.8498		0.8954	
Sample size	30		31	

Notes: All four regressions were tested for heteroscedasticity. The null hypothesis of homoscedasticity for India in 1991 was rejected and hence the weighted least squares approach was employed to re-estimate the model. Standard errors are reported in the parentheses. *, ** and *** represent significance at the level of 1%, 5% and 10%, respectively.

development. As for the level of industrialization, it is not the dominant contributor to regional disparity.[14] In fact, surprisingly, none of the variables representing the level of industrial development is statistically significant. Thus, there may be some room for improvement, e.g. the use of alternative variables. These findings imply that, to reduce regional disparity, governments in China and India should seriously deal with regional differences in the level of infrastructure development and urbanization.

While the findings in Table 3.3 provide important implications, they are subject to several qualifications such as the problems of endogeneity and outliers. The regression results from OLS may be biased due to endogeneity, but lack of data makes it impossible to apply alternative approaches such as the two-stage least squares method. The impact of outliers can, however, be assessed and the results are presented in Table 3.4.[15] The outliers for each dataset were identified by examining the residuals from the regressions in Table 3.3[16]; the regressions excluding the outliers were then re-run. Table 3.4 shows that the explaining power has improved after the exclusion of the outliers in each case. The decomposition of the sources of regional disparity is in general consistent with the results in Table 3.3. That is, infrastructure and urbanization variables still account for the major shares of regional disparity.

3.4 Concluding Remarks

This chapter presents some preliminary findings comparing regional economic growth, disparity and convergence in China

---

[14] Mitra (1992) and Ravallion and Datt (1996) show that industrial growth has had nominal impacts on rural and urban poverty in India.

[15] Only the decomposition results are presented.

[16] It should be pointed out that the choice of outliers was based on an *ad hoc* method that determined the number of outliers to be excluded and in the meantime maintained a reasonable size for the new data sample after the exclusion of the outliers in each case.

Table 3.4   Sensitivity Analysis

Contributing Factors	India		China	
	1991	**2001**	**1990**	**2000**
Infrastructure	10.3	17.4	30.3	59.2
Human capital	6.5	30.1	1.4	
Urbanization	41.6	37.1	35.5	24.3
Industrialization	9.0	3.1	8.9	
Transport/Export	25.4	1.0	11.5	9.7
Total	92.7	88.6	87.6	93.2

Notes: The numbers in the table represent percentage contributions. Three outliers were identified and excluded for the 1991 model (India), one for the 1990 model (China), two for the 2000 model (China) and three for the 2001 model (India). For the 2000 Chinese model, human capital and industrialization variables have insignificant coefficients and are excluded from the final regression.

and India. It is found that regional economic development in China and India is unbalanced. Relatively more developed regions in both countries have forged ahead with no evidence of catch-up by the backward regions. As a result, regional disparity has deteriorated even though the two countries have enjoyed unprecedented growth over the past two decades. In particular, the gap between the super-rich regions and the rest of the economy in both countries has widened since the early 1990s. While regional disparity is generally more severe in China than in India, it has been rising faster in India than in China in recent years. The Chinese government is now fighting hard to reduce regional disparity and build a harmonious society. India will face the same problem if the current trend of rising disparity continues. India could learn from the Chinese experience and try to avoid repeating China's mistakes.

This study also shows that variations in urbanization and infrastructure development are found to be major contributors to regional disparity. While both countries have to build more infrastructure and speed up urbanization, they should also aim for a more balanced strategy among the regions. In addition, it seems that human resource development has also played a role in affecting regional disparity in India in recent years, while in China the export sector is found to be a positive contributor to regional disparity. These findings, though subject to qualifications, may point out the direction for policy responses by governments in China and India in the near future.

Appendix

Sources of data used in this chapter: Chinese statistics are drawn mainly from the *China Statistical Yearbook* compiled by the NBS (various issues). Indian data come from several sources, including the *Handbook of Statistics on the Indian Economy* published by the RBI (2005, 2010); the *Handbook of Urban Statistics* compiled by the National Institute of Urban Affairs, Ministry of Urban Development; and the *Five-Year Plans* formulated by the Planning Commission, Government of India.

Table A3.1   Level of Urbanization in Chinese and Indian Regions

Indian States and Union Territories	Urban Shares (2001, %)	Chinese Regions	Urban Shares (2005, %)
Delhi	93	Shanghai	89
Chandigarh	90	Beijing	84
Pondicherry	67	Tianjin	75
Goa	50	Guangdong	61
Mizoram	50	Liaoning	59
Lakshadweep	44	Zhejiang	56
Tamil Nadu	44	Heilongjiang	53
Maharashtra	42	Jilin	53
Gujarat	37	Jiangsu	50
Daman and Diu	36	Fujian	47
Karnataka	34	Inner Mongolia	47
Punjab	34	Hainan	45
Andaman and Nicobar Islands	33	Chongqing	45

(*Continued*)

Table A3.1 *(Continued)*

Indian States and Union Territories	Urban Shares (2001, %)	Chinese Regions	Urban Shares (2005, %)
Haryana	29	Shandong	45
West Bengal	28	Hubei	43
Andhra Pradesh	27	Ningxia	42
Madhya Pradesh	27	Shanxi	42
Kerala	26	Qinghai	39
Uttaranchal	26	Hebei	38
Jammu and Kashmir	25	Shaanxi	37
Manipur	24	Xinjiang	37
Rajasthan	23	Jiangxi	37
Dadra and Nagar Haveli	23	Hunan	37
Jharkhand	22	Anhui	36
Uttar Pradesh	21	Guangxi	34
Arunachal Pradesh	20	Sichuan	33
Chhattisgarh	20	Henan	31
Meghalaya	20	Gansu	30
Nagaland	18	Yunnan	30
Tripura	17	Guizhou	27
Orissa	15	Tibet	27
Assam	13		
Sikkim	11		
Bihar	10		
Himachal Pradesh	10		
All India	28	All China	43

Notes and sources: Indian data are drawn from the online social statistics database (CSO, 2006). Chinese statistics are drawn from population sampling data reported in NBS (2006).

Table A3.2   Gross Regional Product (GRP) Per Capita in China, 1980–2009

Chinese Regions	1980	1981	1982	1983	1984	1985	1986	1987	1988	1989
Beijing	5,563	5,393	5,658	6,431	7,465	8,001	8,595	9,275	10,300	10,545
Tianjin	3,818	3,949	4,047	4,312	5,079	5,547	5,799	6,155	6,412	6,422
Hebei	1,215	1,209	1,328	1,459	1,648	1,832	1,903	2,093	2,340	2,446
Shanxi	1,314	1,307	1,491	1,671	1,998	2,108	2,210	2,288	2,425	2,508
Inner Mongolia	1,173	1,285	1,502	1,618	1,856	2,152	2,257	2,429	2,633	2,668
Liaoning	2,453	2,385	2,471	2,774	3,200	3,598	3,858	4,346	4,723	4,814
Jilin	1,229	1,285	1,372	1,654	1,851	1,964	2,093	2,466	2,834	2,729
Heilongjiang	2,266	2,337	2,460	2,645	2,915	3,068	3,149	3,386	3,634	3,816
Shanghai	6,524	6,797	7,180	7,638	8,439	9,479	9,784	10,381	11,289	11,511
Jiangsu	1,298	1,425	1,545	1,717	1,973	2,301	2,518	2,829	3,207	3,229
Zhejiang	1,394	1,540	1,693	1,808	2,180	2,633	2,922	3,231	3,550	3,493
Anhui	729	843	912	982	1,169	1,338	1,470	1,521	1,580	1,633
Fujian	1,189	1,353	1,456	1,520	1,769	2,032	2,124	2,374	2,670	2,835
Jiangxi	868	907	980	1,033	1,180	1,323	1,387	1,477	1,623	1,694
Shandong	1,203	1,259	1,382	1,557	1,810	1,998	2,099	2,351	2,604	2,675
Henan	937	995	1,022	1,245	1,353	1,513	1,557	1,759	1,891	1,934
Hubei	1,098	1,155	1,279	1,351	1,608	1,850	1,930	2,067	2,193	2,255

(Continued)

Table A3.2 *(Continued)*

Chinese Regions	1980	1981	1982	1983	1984	1985	1986	1987	1988	1989
Hunan	1,172	1,221	1,314	1,417	1,534	1,701	1,817	1,958	2,079	2,111
Guangdong	1,651	1,756	1,921	2,017	2,283	2,694	2,964	3,409	4,596	4,119
Guangxi	896	946	1,045	1,062	1,117	1,216	1,270	1,364	1,394	1,420
Hainan						1,794	1,841	1,987	2,152	2,234
Chongqing	958	998	1,071	1,158	1,326	1,448	1,552	1,606	1,734	1,813
Sichuan	1,020	1,029	1,136	1,227	1,411	1,626	1,685	1,781	1,878	1,819
Guizhou	656	685	779	866	1,028	1,098	1,144	1,250	1,327	1,367
Yunnan	962	1,022	1,163	1,238	1,401	1,561	1,604	1,770	2,021	2,105
Tibet					1,772	2,001	1,793	1,761	1,792	1,906
Shaanxi	1,008	1,044	1,123	1,193	1,393	1,606	1,727	1,864	2,222	2,255
Gansu	958	865	930	1,056	1,155	1,327	1,453	1,560	1,747	1,871
Qinghai	1,618	1,575	1,726	1,878	2,109	2,282	2,402	2,500	2,631	2,626
Ningxia	1,402	1,392	1,478	1,673	1,868	2,158	2,288	2,410	2,639	2,782
Xinjiang	1,455	1,552	1,683	1,894	2,142	2,484	2,715	2,949	3,186	3,315

(Continued)

Table A3.2 *(Continued)*

Chinese Regions	1990	1991	1992	1993	1994	1995	1996	1997	1998	1999
Beijing	10,985	11,914	13,218	14,357	15,707	17,080	18,086	18,991	20,099	21,110
Tianjin	6,661	6,975	7,733	8,558	9,666	11,027	12,464	13,937	15,042	16,354
Hebei	2,470	2,702	3,094	3,620	4,122	4,658	5,247	5,863	6,472	7,075
Shanxi	2,593	2,659	2,986	3,442	3,778	3,947	4,334	4,753	5,094	4,818
Inner Mongolia	2,822	2,992	3,288	3,564	3,840	4,104	4,534	4,833	5,228	5,444
Liaoning	4,819	5,080	5,660	6,469	7,151	7,609	8,238	8,702	9,522	10,362
Jilin	2,774	2,902	3,234	3,620	4,062	4,402	4,978	5,304	5,871	6,455
Heilongjiang	3,993	4,230	4,476	4,793	5,187	5,656	6,214	6,802	7,371	7,784
Shanghai	11,811	12,600	14,445	16,462	18,659	21,128	23,725	26,584	29,054	31,677
Jiangsu	3,270	3,647	4,531	5,379	6,219	7,126	7,945	8,847	9,771	10,711
Zhejiang	3,601	4,215	4,988	5,997	7,151	8,285	9,286	10,246	11,191	12,229
Anhui	1,637	1,580	1,820	2,245	2,940	3,263	3,733	4,255	4,462	4,652
Fujian	2,974	3,319	3,950	4,970	6,049	6,940	8,041	9,050	10,259	10,875
Jiangxi	1,740	1,855	2,150	2,362	2,734	3,117	3,709	4,095	4,442	4,672
Shandong	2,744	3,069	3,563	4,339	5,049	5,760	6,458	7,178	7,922	8,733
Henan	1,983	2,085	2,342	2,689	3,038	3,463	3,946	4,309	4,673	5,001
Hubei	2,317	2,420	2,724	3,074	3,533	3,966	4,802	5,470	5,988	6,398

(Continued)

Table A3.2   (*Continued*)

Chinese Regions	1990	1991	1992	1993	1994	1995	1996	1997	1998	1999
Hunan	2,161	2,302	2,568	2,963	3,265	3,600	4,049	4,496	4,928	5,176
Guangdong	4,466	5,105	6,123	6,845	7,897	8,827	10,120	10,787	11,565	12,288
Guangxi	1,492	1,655	1,932	2,367	2,726	3,214	3,602	3,919	3,839	4,080
Hainan	2,438	2,738	3,781	4,462	5,129	5,300	5,450	5,710	6,079	6,486
Chongqing	1,732	1,857	2,219	2,600	2,920	3,456	3,705	4,177	4,480	4,795
Sichuan	1,919	2,102	2,403	2,758	2,986	3,338	3,653	3,988	4,311	4,511
Guizhou	1,397	1,483	1,611	1,748	1,869	1,977	2,139	2,214	2,387	2,502
Yunnan	2,244	2,349	2,567	2,792	3,058	3,347	3,631	3,910	4,164	4,400
Tibet	2,319	2,027	2,137	2,274	2,583	3,010	3,359	3,687	3,988	4,329
Shaanxi	2,282	2,402	2,581	2,778	2,954	3,160	3,461	3,798	4,015	4,261
Gansu	1,925	2,012	2,170	2,391	2,606	2,768	3,021	3,236	3,480	3,715
Qinghai	2,683	2,765	2,924	3,162	3,376	3,545	3,832	4,116	4,424	4,713
Ningxia	2,786	2,861	3,050	3,302	3,464	3,641	3,895	4,084	4,302	4,544
Xinjiang	3,541	3,858	4,296	4,691	5,094	5,439	5,677	6,227	6,622	7,008

(*Continued*)

Table A3.2 (*Continued*)

Chinese Regions	2000	2001	2002	2003	2004	2005	2006	2007	2008	2009
Beijing	22,460	24,288	25,870	27,891	33,817	36,448	39,269	42,751	44,745	50,408
Tianjin	17,993	20,023	22,351	25,386	28,082	30,079	34,734	38,190	41,834	49,107
Hebei	7,663	8,310	9,105	10,186	10,050	12,682	14,408	16,050	17,557	18,978
Shanxi	5,137	5,413	6,005	6,766	9,044	10,079	11,144	12,549	13,498	14,923
Inner Mongolia	5,872	6,419	7,279	8,285	11,499	14,181	16,380	19,032	21,502	27,417
Liaoning	11,226	12,173	12,877	14,858	16,733	18,758	21,265	24,068	27,084	31,027
Jilin	7,012	7,169	7,731	8,418	9,955	11,134	12,770	14,788	17,114	19,413
Heilongjiang	8,562	9,499	10,632	11,986	12,246	13,652	15,242	17,031	19,129	21,317
Shanghai	34,547	37,828	41,561	45,989	43,214	46,682	51,581	57,839	62,080	67,849
Jiangsu	11,773	12,874	14,275	16,137	18,490	20,741	23,917	27,040	29,887	34,109
Zhejiang	13,309	14,435	16,101	18,224	21,009	23,404	26,182	29,543	32,070	34,478
Anhui	4,867	5,081	5,699	6,232	6,926	7,724	8,816	10,015	11,287	12,697
Fujian	11,601	12,416	13,613	15,128	16,056	17,837	20,380	23,231	26,081	29,102
Jiangxi	4,851	5,174	5,670	6,403	7,139	8,000	8,648	9,519	10,490	12,671
Shandong	9,555	10,442	11,617	13,143	17,894	16,875	19,219	21,792	24,198	26,882
Henan	5,444	5,897	6,624	7,315	8,111	9,285	10,673	12,115	13,845	14,930
Hubei	7,188	8,242	8,572	9,281	9,585	10,607	12,083	13,775	15,771	17,865

(*Continued*)

Table A3.2 (*Continued*)

Chinese Regions	2000	2001	2002	2003	2004	2005	2006	2007	2008	2009
Hunan	5,639	6,118	6,862	7,490	8,423	9,195	10,199	11,586	13,033	15,287
Guangdong	12,885	13,535	14,802	16,639	19,451	21,736	24,546	27,612	29,849	33,421
Guangxi	4,319	4,613	5,325	5,800	6,666	7,653	8,551	9,781	10,909	12,054
Hainan	6,894	7,342	7,567	8,354	9,714	10,312	11,677	12,958	14,073	16,012
Chongqing	5,157	5,614	6,168	6,839	8,646	8,558	9,684	11,037	12,541	16,256
Sichuan	4,883	5,305	5,881	6,577	7,773	8,884	9,465	10,901	12,097	13,906
Guizhou	2,662	2,861	3,097	3,395	3,854	4,253	4,711	5,241	6,028	7,141
Yunnan	4,637	4,889	5,243	5,629	6,454	6,992	7,754	8,543	9,460	10,524
Tibet	4,724	4,824	5,481	6,098	6,913	7,719	8,564	9,653	10,520	11,673
Shaanxi	4,549	4,949	5,566	6,159	7,506	7,942	9,198	10,561	12,086	14,612
Gansu	3,838	4,276	4,630	5,006	6,005	6,777	7,518	8,403	9,241	10,129
Qinghai	5,087	5,629	6,228	6,887	7,735	8,603	9,563	10,700	11,595	13,455
Ningxia	4,839	5,139	5,508	6,055	7,681	8,314	9,149	10,070	10,573	12,810
Xinjiang	7,377	7,853	8,321	9,144	10,179	11,071	12,026	13,217	14,460	15,326

Notes and sources: Author's own estimation using raw data from the NBS (various issues). Blank cells indicate missing data. The unit is yuan in 2000 constant prices.

Table A3.3 Gross Regional Product (GRP) Per Capita in India, 1980/81–2009/10

(Based On 1980–1981 Constant Prices)

Indian States and Union Territories	1980–81	1981–82	1982–83	1983–84	1984–85	1985–86	1986–87
Andhra Pradesh	1,380	1,569	1,563	1,593	1,512	1,573	1,497
Arunachal Pradesh	1,571	1,750	1,755	1,821	1,937	2,119	2,195
Assam	1,284	1,402	1,437	1,470	1,447	1,510	1,437
Bihar	917	947	935	1,003	1,074	1,074	1,135
Jharkhand							
Goa	3,145	2,866	3,239	3,214	3,283	3,091	3,196
Gujarat	1,940	2,084	2,008	2,343	2,293	2,186	2,276
Haryana	2,370	2,399	2,487	2,479	2,513	2,893	2,825
Himachal Pradesh	1,704	1,773	1,678	1,726	1,599	1,781	1,877
Jammu and Kashmir	1,776	1,772	1,782	1,794	1,837	1,832	1,809
Karnataka	1,520	1,583	1,586	1,663	1,750	1,644	1,764
Kerala	1,508	1,469	1,485	1,406	1,473	1,507	1,453
Madhya Pradesh	1,358	1,360	1,388	1,427	1,327	1,409	1,315
Chhattisgarh							
Maharashtra	2,435	2,441	2,480	2,579	2,558	2,705	2,666
Manipur	1,419	1,462	1,447	1,530	1,553	1,598	1,588

(*Continued*)

Table A3,3 (*Continued*)

(Based On 1980–1981 Constant Prices)

Indian States and Union Territories	1980–81	1981–82	1982–83	1983–84	1984–85	1985–86	1986–87
Meghalaya	1,361	1,379	1,361	1,354	1,385	1,412	1,397
Mizoram							
Nagaland	1,361	1,577	1,720	1,695	1,681	1,653	1,768
Orissa	1,314	1,290	1,191	1,407	1,316	1,442	1,436
Punjab	2,674	2,875	2,906	2,904	3,073	3,249	3,302
Rajasthan	1,222	1,285	1,276	1,525	1,379	1,338	1,428
Sikkim	1,571	1,611	1,750	1,758	1,919	2,017	2,297
Tamil Nadu	1,498	1,640	1,527	1,582	1,758	1,798	1,755
Tripura	1,307	1,248	1,339	1,261	1,262	1,240	1,274
Uttar Pradesh	1,278	1,276	1,344	1,364	1,354	1,375	1,402
Uttarakhand							
West Bengal	1,773	1,689	1,719	1,883	1,892	1,929	1,962
Andaman and Nicobar Islands	2,613	2,604	2,414	2,660	2,445	2,639	2,644
Chandigarh							
Delhi	4,030	4,163	4,495	4,206	4,201	4,665	4,765
Puducherry	2,794	2,758	2,898	2,847	2,923	2,976	3,067

(*Continued*)

Table A3.3 *(Continued)*

(Based On 1980–1981 Constant Prices)

Indian States and Union Territories	1987–88	1988–89	1989–90	1990–91	1991–92	1992–93	1993–94
Andhra Pradesh	1,663	1,906	2,013	2,060	2,134	2,039	2,232
Arunachal Pradesh	2,265	2,374	2,363	2,709	3,013	3,015	3,368
Assam	1,468	1,446	1,517	1,544	1,575	1,557	1,583
Bihar	1,050	1,158	1,116	1,197	1,105	1,017	1,019
Jharkhand							
Goa	3,498	4,195	4,328	4,883	4,786	5,381	5,497
Gujarat	1,986	2,737	2,644	2,641	2,381	3,091	2,944
Haryana	2,709	3,289	3,254	3,509	3,499	3,421	3,498
Himachal Pradesh	1,850	2,046	2,250	2,241	2,213	2,267	2,315
Jammu and Kashmir	1,571	1,736	1,730	1,784	1,779	1,816	1,861
Karnataka	1,853	1,978	2,055	2,039	2,262	2,278	2,410
Kerala	1,482	1,614	1,705	1,815	1,826	1,932	2,103
Madhya Pradesh	1,459	1,529	1,523	1,696	1,538	1,618	1,754
Chhattisgarh							
Maharashtra	2,781	3,000	3,414	3,483	3,399	3,837	4,177
Manipur	1,669	1,707	1,687	1,739	1,841	1,886	1,881

(Continued)

Table A3.3   *(Continued)*

(Based On 1980–1981 Constant Prices)

Indian States and Union Territories	1987–88	1988–89	1989–90	1990–91	1991–92	1992–93	1993–94
Meghalaya	1,485	1,455	1,596	1,733	1,764	1,617	1,681
Mizoram							
Nagaland	1,907	1,983	1,986	1,976	2,006	2,239	2,170
Orissa	1,365	1,623	1,699	1,383	1,530	1,476	1,543
Punjab	3,410	3,526	3,730	3,730	3,825	3,931	4,026
Rajasthan	1,295	1,791	1,716	1,942	1,755	1,975	1,776
Sikkim	2,678	2,924	3,118	3,369	3,492		
Tamil Nadu	1,837	1,987	2,094	2,237	2,270	2,363	2,544
Tripura	1,398	1,523	1,575	1,642	1,643	1,666	1,808
Uttar Pradesh	1,433	1,584	1,593	1,652	1,627	1,615	1,626
Uttarakhand							
West Bengal	2,022	2,061	2,086	2,145	2,267	2,295	2,419
Andaman and Nicobar Islands	2,695	2,817	2,715	2,580	2,302	2,884	3,094
Chandigarh							
Delhi	4,975	5,185	5,438	5,447	6,046	6,042	6,238
Puducherry	3,003	3,055	3,100	3,183	2,883	2,434	2,766

(Continued)

Table A3.3   *(Continued)*

Indian States and Union Territories	1993–94	1994–95	1995–96	1996–97	1997–98	1998–99	1999–2000
			(Based On 1993–1994 Constant Prices)				
Andhra Pradesh	7,416	7,711	8,071	8,514	8,191	9,144	9,445
Arunachal Pradesh	8,733	8,342	9,352	8,590	8,634	8,712	8,890
Assam	5,715	5,737	5,760	5,793	5,796	5,684	5,785
Bihar	3,037	3,306	2,728	3,338	3,100	3,210	3,282
Jharkhand	5,897	6,050	6,105	5,647	7,259	7,754	7,238
Goa	16,558	16,977	17,929	20,686	20,595	25,364	25,371
Gujarat	9,796	11,535	11,649	13,206	13,018	13,735	13,298
Haryana	11,079	11,598	11,545	12,591	12,389	12,728	13,308
Himachal Pradesh	7,870	8,489	8,801	9,140	9,625	10,131	11,051
Jammu and Kashmir	6,543	6,619	6,732	6,978	7,128	7,296	7,384
Karnataka	7,838	8,097	8,368	8,990	9,416	10,549	10,912
Kerala	7,983	8,598	8,868	9,145	9,265	9,819	10,430
Madhya Pradesh	6,584	6,550	6,790	7,089	7,301	7,621	8,248
Chhattisgarh	6,539	6,445	6,474	6,654	6,810	6,873	6,692
Maharashtra	12,183	12,158	13,221	13,464	13,925	14,199	15,257
Manipur	5,846	5,558	5,616	6,022	6,434	6,401	7,097

(Continued)

Table A3.3 (*Continued*)

(Based On 1993–1994 Constant Prices)

Indian States and Union Territories	1993–94	1994–95	1995–96	1996–97	1997–98	1998–99	1999–2000
Meghalaya	6,893	6,940	7,535	7,602	7,881	8,507	8,996
Mizoram							
Nagaland	9,129	9,410	9,646	9,880	10,287	9,118	8,726
Orissa	4,896	5,054	5,204	4,773	5,382	5,471	5,742
Punjab	12,710	12,784	13,008	13,705	13,812	14,334	14,809
Rajasthan	6,182	7,134	7,216	7,862	8,601	8,754	8,555
Sikkim	8,402	8,277	8,822	9,146	9,539	9,914	9,874
Tamil Nadu	8,955	9,932	10,147	10,451	11,260	11,592	12,167
Tripura	5,534	5,364	5,707	6,239	6,828	7,396	7,968
Uttar Pradesh	5,066	5,209	5,256	5,706	5,518	5,432	5,675
Uttarakhand	6,896	7,369	7,163	7,476	7,429	7,385	7,256
West Bengal	6,756	7,094	7,492	7,880	8,408	8,814	9,320
Andaman and Nicobar Islands	15,192	16,191	15,354	15,896	16,350	14,502	15,293
Chandigarh	19,761	21,021	22,524	24,855	25,470	26,718	27,494
Delhi	18,166	19,575	19,162	20,983	23,482	23,762	24,003
Puducherry	9,781	9,661	9,889	13,512	17,402	19,279	19,374

(*Continued*)

Table A3.3   (*Continued*)

(Based On 1999–2000 Constant Prices)

Indian States and Union Territories	1999–2000	2000–01	2001–02	2002–03	2003–04	2004–05	2005–06
Andhra Pradesh	15,427	16,574	17,213	17,340	18,819	19,963	21,728
Arunachal Pradesh	13,990	14,726	16,793	15,832	17,340	19,339	18,179
Assam	12,282	12,447	12,529	13,072	13,675	13,946	14,419
Bihar	5,786	6,554	5,994	6,658	6,117	6,772	6,745
Jharkhand	11,549	9,980	10,451	10,563	11,173	12,869	12,950
Goa	42,296	38,989	39,339	40,602	42,206	45,394	52,201
Gujarat	18,864	17,227	18,200	19,509	22,387	23,346	26,268
Haryana	23,222	24,423	25,638	26,748	28,805	30,690	32,980
Himachal Pradesh	20,806	21,824	22,543	23,234	24,377	26,244	27,447
Jammu and Kashmir	13,816	13,859	13,784	14,341	14,848	15,414	16,086
Karnataka	17,502	17,352	17,402	18,115	18,236	19,840	22,322
Kerala	19,461	19,809	20,659	21,944	23,159	25,122	27,714
Madhya Pradesh	12,384	11,150	11,715	10,880	11,870	12,032	12,567
Chhattisgarh	11,629	10,808	12,202	11,716	13,661	14,070	14,694
Maharashtra	23,011	21,892	22,258	23,447	24,859	26,603	28,683
Manipur	13,260	12,157	12,641	12,319	13,389	14,334	14,663

(*Continued*)

Table A3.3 *(Continued)*

(Based On 1999–2000 Constant Prices)

Indian States and Union Territories	1999–2000	2000–01	2001–02	2002–03	2003–04	2004–05	2005–06
Meghalaya	14,355	14,910	15,518	15,882	16,658	17,595	18,870
Mizoram	16,443	16,635	17,245	18,429	18,555	18,904	18,616
Nagaland	14,107	15,699	16,637	17,409	17,319	17,269	17,008
Orissa	10,622	10,208	10,697	10,500	11,900	13,311	13,877
Punjab	25,631	25,986	25,992	25,955	27,075	27,905	28,487
Rajasthan	13,619	12,840	13,933	12,054	15,579	14,908	15,736
Sikkim	14,890	15,305	15,953	17,065	18,159	19,332	20,777
Tamil Nadu	19,432	20,319	19,748	19,662	20,707	22,975	25,558
Tripura	14,119	14,933	16,947	17,752	18,554	19,825	21,524
Uttar Pradesh	9,749	9,721	9,672	9,806	10,120	10,421	10,758
Uttarakhand	13,516	14,932	15,364	16,530	17,542	19,524	20,219
West Bengal	15,888	16,244	17,225	17,568	18,374	19,367	20,187
Andaman and Nicobar Islands	24,005	23,658	23,869	25,487	27,229	27,267	28,752
Chandigarh	44,502	48,292	50,476	55,991	59,406	62,352	65,218
Delhi	38,913	38,975	39,026	40,929	41,930	45,157	48,885
Puducherry	30,486	34,190	35,831	38,648	39,633	33,585	35,856

(Continued)

Table A3.3 *(Continued)*

(Based On 1999–2000 Constant Prices)

Indian States and Union Territories	2006–07	2007–08	2008–09	2009–10
Andhra Pradesh	23,898	26,229	27,362	28,384
Arunachal Pradesh	20,458	21,582	22,475	
Assam	14,894	15,526	16,272	17,080
Bihar	8,233	8,818	10,206	10,577
Jharkhand	14,252	15,303	16,294	
Goa	56,021	60,232		
Gujarat	28,335	31,780		
Haryana	36,669	39,462	41,896	44,493
Himachal Pradesh	28,620	30,519	32,343	
Jammu and Kashmir	16,817	17,590		
Karnataka	23,593	26,418	27,385	
Kerala	30,476	33,372	35,457	
Madhya Pradesh	12,881	13,299		
Chhattisgarh	17,059	18,770	19,521	21,359
Maharashtra	30,982	33,302		
Manipur	14,941	15,667	16,508	

(Continued)

Table A3.3 *(Continued)*

(Based On 1999–2000 Constant Prices)

Indian States and Union Territories	2006–07	2007–08	2008–09	2009–10
Meghalaya	20,185	21,597	23,069	
Mizoram	19,220	19,750		19,456
Nagaland	17,129			34,935
Orissa	15,760	17,352	18,212	19,806
Punjab	30,154	31,662	33,198	
Rajasthan	17,480	18,769	19,708	
Sikkim	22,277	23,684	25,257	
Tamil Nadu	28,320	29,445	30,652	
Tripura	21,706	22,493		
Uttar Pradesh	11,334	11,939	12,481	
Uttarakhand	21,816	23,477	25,114	
West Bengal	21,773	23,456	24,720	
Andaman and Nicobar Islands	30,551	31,626		
Chandigarh	71,129	75,674	77,801	
Delhi	54,821	60,189		
Puducherry	49,303	55,808	58,755	

Notes and sources: Raw data drawn from the RBI (2010). Blank cells indicate missing data. The unit is rupee.

Chapter 4

Role of the Service Sector

Aggregate and regional growth in China and India has been explored in the preceding two chapters. This chapter presents a case study at the sector level. A comparison of the economic structure in the two countries demonstrates that the role of the service sector — or the tertiary sector, as it is known in China — in the two economies is very different (see Figure 4.1). On the one hand, the service sector has become the dominant contributor to the Indian economy, accounting for 59.3% of GDP during the 2008/2009 financial year.[1] The success in this sector is regarded as "India's services revolution" (Gordon and Gupta, 2004). On the other hand, China's service sector has lagged well behind the manufacturing sector (or the secondary sector according to Chinese terminology), and its role in the economy has improved only slightly in the last 15 years when the Chinese economy achieved its best performance in recent history. During 1990–2009, for example, the service sector GDP as a proportion of China's GDP increased modestly from 38.8% in 1990 to 41.6% in 2009, according to Figure 4.1. Why have the two countries taken very different trajectories in developing their service economies? What are the implications for future developments in the two Asian giants? Which factors affect demand for services in China and India? These are some of the questions that will be investigated in this chapter.

---

[1] See Table A2.2 in the Appendix to Chapter 2 for details.

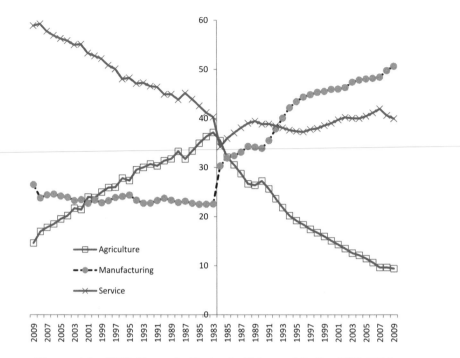

Figure 4.1   GDP Shares by Sector in China and India, 1983–2009

Notes and sources: Author's own drawing on the basis of data from Table A2.2 in the Appendix to Chapter 2. The vertical axis represents percentage income shares by sector. China is represented on the right-hand side of the diagram and India on the left-hand side.

There is hardly any comparative study of services in China and India.[2] However, several studies have focused on the service sector in individual countries. For example, Gupta (1998) and Mohan (1998) examine productivity in India's service sector in comparison with other Asian economies, Chanda (2002) discusses service trade in the world particularly in India and its implications for World Trade Organization (WTO) negotiations in services, and Gordon and Gupta (2004) present a detailed study explaining India's service growth in the past decade.

[2] Exceptions are several comparative studies on banking (Shanker *et al.*, 2009; Shirai, 2002) and service outsourcing (Soo, 2005).

Examples of studies on China include Li and Hou's (2003) edited volume on China's WTO entry and its implications for the service sector, Jiang's (2004) edited book focusing on growth and structural changes in services in China with some marginal coverage of international comparisons, and Li's (2004a, 2004b) comprehensive investigation of China's service sector. This study extends the existing literature by comparing growth in and demand for services in China and India.

The rest of this chapter begins with a brief review of developments in the service sector in China and India (Section 4.1). This is followed by a discussion of the determinants of the demand for services (Section 4.2). Three empirical models are employed to examine the factors affecting demand for services internationally as well as in China and India. Subsequently, the chapter discusses the growth outlook of services in the two countries (Section 4.3). The final section (Section 4.4) summarizes the findings.

4.1 Service Sector Development

Following the conventional classification, an economy is divided into three sectors: agriculture (or primary), manufacturing (or secondary) and service (or tertiary) sectors. The agricultural sector consists of farming, forestry, animal husbandry and fishery. The manufacturing sector is composed of mining, construction and manufacturing.[3] All other economic activities that are not covered by the agricultural and manufacturing sectors are broadly defined as services and hence belong to the service sector. These include services provided for the agricultural sector, activities associated

---

[3] Whether services include construction and public utilities is controversial (Ochel and Wegner, 1987). According to the Indian classification as well as the World Bank (2005), construction and public utilities are treated as part of services. However, the Chinese classification excludes construction and public utilities from services. The OECD (2005) also excludes construction from services. This book follows the OECD system, which includes construction in the manufacturing category.

with the supply of water, electricity and gas, transport and communications, wholesale and retail trade, finance and insurance, business and personal services, and community and social services. Services can be broadly distinguished between two types, that is, old and new services. Old or traditional services include petty trading, domestic services, catering and hotel services. New services are generally associated with communications, business and legal practice, culture, research and education.[4] The latter are tradable internationally and hence are also called tradable services.

4.1.1 *Service Sector Growth*

The service sector in both countries has achieved high growth, with an average annual growth rate of 10.7% in China and 7.4% in India during the period 1979–2009.[5] The gap between the growth rates matches the difference in the rates of GDP growth in the two countries. During the same period, an average annual GDP growth rate of 9.8% was recorded for the Chinese economy while the same rate was 5.7% for India.[6]

At the disaggregate level, the structure of the service sector in China and India is very similar. It is still dominated by the traditional or old services, followed by business services (finance, insurance and real estate) and transport and communications, according to Table 4.1. However, the new service sectors are catching up rapidly. During 1999–2003, communication services achieved the strongest growth in both countries (with an average annual growth rate of 16.77% in China and 23.89% in India), followed by education (8.59%) and research (11.94%) in India and real estate (8.75%) and research (8.93%)

---

[4] Luo (2001) provides a detailed survey of the main service sectors, especially the new service sectors, in China.

[5] India's growth rate is based on the financial years 1979/1980–2009/2010 (RBI, 2010). The Chinese rate is calculated using data from the NBS (various issues).

[6] These growth rates are derived using data from the RBI (2010) and NBS (various issues).

Table 4.1 Composition of Service Sector GDP (2003, %)

Service Sectors	China	India	Australia	Korea	Japan	UK	US
Finance and insurance	16.50	13.27	11.83	15.53	9.78	6.89	10.35
Government and social organizations	8.01	10.78	6.06	10.47	6.72	6.62	10.35
Real estate	6.07	11.64	29.15	22.34	30.66	32.16	30.92
Wholesale, retail trade and catering	23.57	30.39	19.15	17.98	18.54	20.81	20.05
Transport, telecommunications, etc.	16.96	19.18	12.11	13.09	8.91	10.00	7.89
Transport and storage	8.76	10.86					
Post and telecommunications	8.20	8.32					
Education, health, research, etc.	28.87	14.73	21.69	20.59	25.40	23.51	20.44
Education, culture and arts	8.71	7.98					
Health, sports and social welfare	2.96	2.14					
Scientific research and polytechnic	2.25	0.89					
Others	14.95	3.71					
Total	100	100	100	100	100	100	100

Notes and sources: China's "Others" category may contain items which belong to the "Wholesale, Retail Trade and Catering" group. Data are drawn from the NBS (various issues), OECD (2005) and CSO (2005).

in China.[7] Though growing rapidly in recent years, research-related services are still relatively small in both countries according to Table 4.1. The same table also shows that, in comparison with other major economies, services in the areas of real estate, health, sports and social welfare in both China and India are relatively weak.

4.1.2 *Output and Employment Shares*

The development of the service sector can also be examined by analyzing the sectoral shares of output and employment over the national totals in the two countries. Output shares of the service sector in China and India have grown steadily since 1978, as shown in Figure 4.2.[8] The role of services in the Indian economy is clearly more significant than that of services in the Chinese economy. Accordingly, since 1990, India's service sector has grown faster (at an annual rate of 8.0%) than the manufacturing sector (at an annual rate of 6.7%); while the opposite is true in China, where the manufacturing sector (with an average rate of growth of 12.0%) has outpaced the growth of the service sector (at a rate of 9.8%).[9]

In contrast, the employment share of India's service sector is much smaller than its income share, according to statistics covering the period 1983–2009 (Figure 4.3). This share has nevertheless enjoyed steady growth. In particular, growth in India's service employment share in the 2000s (2.69% annually during 2000–2009) was much faster than in the 1980s and 1990s (1.20% annually). In comparison with India, the service

---

[7] These rates of growth are calculated using data from the CSO (2005) and NBS (various issues).

[8] China's figures are based on the recently released economic survey results (http://www.stats.gov.cn), which show that service activities were previously substantially underreported.

[9] These growth rates are based on data from the RBI (2005) and NBS (various issues) including China's recently released economic survey results.

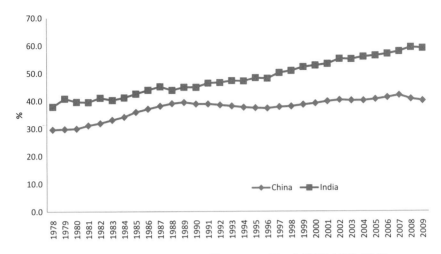

Figure 4.2   Service Sector Share over Total GDP, 1978–2009

Notes and sources: Data are drawn from the NBS (various issues) and RBI (2010).

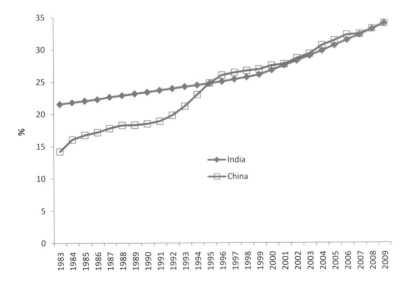

Figure 4.3   Employment Shares of the Service Sectors, 1983–2009

Notes and sources: Data are drawn from Table A2.2 in the Appendix to Chapter 2.

employment share in China recorded a slower growth in the 2000s (2.38% annually) than in the 1980s and 1990s (with an average annual rate of growth of 3.53% during 1985–1999). As a result, by 2009 the two countries' shares of service employment were similar even though India's share was much higher than China's in the early 1980s.

4.1.3 *Regional Variations*

In terms of the level of development of the service sector, there is considerable variation across the regions in both countries.[10] Several observations can be made. First, regional development in services follows the national trend. In general, the service sectors at the regional level in India are on average more developed than those in China. For example, China's most advanced service sector is in Beijing which had a GDP share of 72% in 2007, while India's most advanced service sector is in Delhi with a GDP share of 84% in the same year, according to Figures 4.4 and 4.5.[11] Second, the service sector tends to be more important among relatively more developed regions in both countries. Figures 4.4 and 4.5 clearly show a positive relationship between the level of service sector development and GDP per capita in both Chinese and Indian regions. Finally, the service sector plays a more important role in regions where the level of urbanization is high, such as Delhi and Chandigarh in India as well as Beijing and Shanghai in China.

4.1.4 *Growth from an International Perspective*

The experience of economic development shows that, when a country expands its manufacturing capacity, the primary sector in the

---

[10] Wong and Liang (2003a) examine regional variation in China's service development.

[11] The service sectors at the regional level in China are likely to be underreported, given the fact that data at the national level have been substantially underreported. However, regional revised data are not yet available.

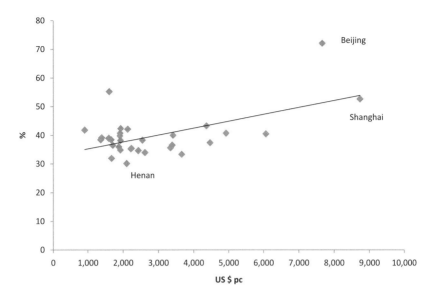

Figure 4.4 GDP Per Capita and Service Sector GDP Shares in Chinese Regions, 2007

Notes and sources: Data are drawn from the NBS (2008). The straight line represents the fitted regression line. In 2007, US$1 = 7.6 Chinese yuan.

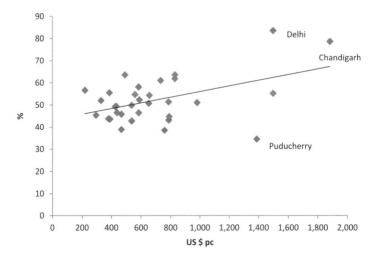

Figure 4.5 GDP Per Capita and Service Sector GDP Shares in Indian Regions, 2007

Notes and sources: Data are drawn from the RBI (2010). The straight line represents the fitted regression line. During the 2007/2008 financial year, US$1 = 40.2 rupees.

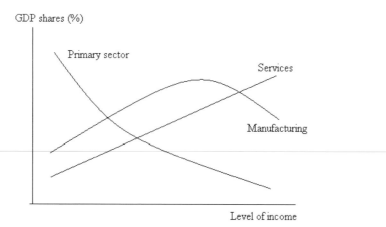

Figure 4.6   Economic Structure and Level of Development

economy will decline relatively, but over time the service sector will grow and eventually overtake the manufacturing sector to become the dominant part of the economy (Figure 4.6). For example, the GDP share of services over national total in 2007 amounted to 69% in Australia, 76% in the United Kingdom and 77% in the United States (World Bank, 2010). The change process in these countries has followed the stages of economic development. However, from an international perspective, China's service sector development is lagging behind the world's average trend while India's is slightly above the average. This is clearly demonstrated in Figure 4.7, which illustrates service sector GDP shares against per capita income among nations at a similar stage of development. Information at the disaggregate level also implies that services in China and India are still at the early stage of development, as represented by the dominance of old services and the weakness of real estate, education and research services (Table 4.1).

The relative backwardness of services in China is also reflected in the role of service trade. In 2003, China was the world's fourth largest merchandise exporter but its service export was only ranked 10th (World Bank, 2005). The share of service exports over total exports in China (9.6% in 2003) was much smaller than in the United States (28.4%), the United

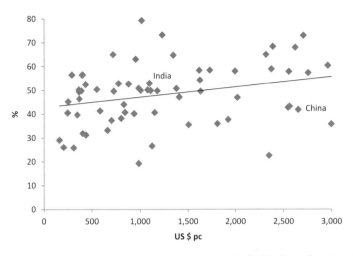

Figure 4.7 Service Sector GDP Shares and GDP Per Capita Across Countries, 2007

Notes and sources: Data are drawn from the World Development Indicators online database (http://www.worldbank.org).

Kingdom (32.4%), Australia (22.4%), Japan (13.9%) and the world as a whole (18.6%) during the same period.[12] Not surprisingly, China is currently a net importer of services. In contrast, India's service exports accounted for 30.9% of total exports in 2003, making the country a net exporter of services according to the World Bank (2005). This is largely due to India's success in information technology (IT) service exports and India's relatively small value of merchandise exports, which was equivalent to only 12% of China's in 2003. In 2003, India's total merchandise export was ranked 31st in the world but its service export was ranked 20th (World Bank, 2005). Moreover, among the service exports, the finance and insurance share in 2003 only amounted to 1.0% and 1.5% in China and India, respectively, while this share was 7.8% in the United States and 22.6% in the United Kingdom in the same year (World Bank, 2005).

---

[12] These shares are derived using data from the World Bank (2005).

4.2 Determinants of Service Growth

4.2.1 *The Theory*

It is argued that growth of the service sector is determined by several factors such as production specialization, income level and urbanization (Mulder, 2001; Wolfl, 2005). These factors are interrelated: as an economy grows, productive activities become more specialized, and urbanization accelerates due to the rising level of income. In the meantime, as a result of the increasing specialization of production, firms tend to outsource many service activities such as legal, accounting and security services. Some authors call this process of specialization "splintering" (Bhagwati, 1984). It is the main source of demand for services from producers.

At the household level, Engel's law states that, as income rises, consumption of food and durable goods in turn becomes saturated over time and demand for services such as healthcare, transport and communications increases. Growth in income also boosts demand for away-from-home consumption of food and services.

Furthermore, urbanization contributes to the growth of the service sector in two ways. Unlike farmers who to some extent can provide self-services, urban consumers rely on the market for the supply of services. They are also more likely to enter the urban informal sector for employment if there are no job opportunities in the formal sector; and services account for the lion's share of the informal sector. Thus, urban residents are both consumers and suppliers of services. It is expected that the service sector will grow as the level of urbanization increases in a society.

In addition, regulatory policies also affect the development of the service sector. A good example is the rapid growth of telecommunications services after deregulation in many countries (Wirtz, 2000). This phenomenon can be repeated in other areas such as insurance, banking, healthcare and so on. Regulatory environments can also affect international trade and foreign investment in services (Mulder, 2001). Finally, the participation of women in the workforce has an impact on service demand as well. The presence of more women in the workforce will inevitably lead to an increase in demand for services, ranging from babysitting and catering to tuition and beauty treatments.

4.2.2 *The Empirics*

To examine the determinants of growth in services in China and India, three models are considered; and they are applied to Chinese provincial, Indian state and cross-country databases, respectively. The econometric model can be expressed as follows:

$$SER = \alpha + \Sigma \beta_j X_j + \varepsilon, \tag{4.1}$$

where SER and X represent demand for services and a list of factors affecting service demand, respectively, α and β are coefficients to be estimated, and ε is the standard error term. Equation (4.1) can be applied to either panel data for the individual country models or cross-section data for cross-country analysis. For panel data models, several optional models are considered, e.g. model without group dummy (the same intercept for all groups), fixed effects model (different intercepts for each group) and random effects model (intercepts that vary by a random error).

SER in Equation (4.1) is measured as the GDP share of services. The choice of the variables (X) in the models is dictated by the availability of data. In the three optional models considered here, X includes per capita income (I), urbanization (U), service export shares in total exports (EX) and the proportion of women in the total non-farming workforce (W). EX and W are not available for the regions of China and India, and hence are incorporated only in the cross-country model. The Chinese data cover 31 regions over the period 1993–2003. The Indian statistics are available for 31 (out of 35) states and union territories for nine years (1993–2001). The cross-country database has one-year (2003) data for 93 countries. The estimation results are reported in Table 4.2.

According to Table 4.2, the estimated coefficients of both per capita income (I) and urbanization (U) are positive and statistically

Table 4.2   Estimation Results

	Fixed Effects	**Random Effects**
Chinese model		
Income per capita	0.00059 (6.20)*	0.00059 (6.32)*
Urbanization	0.15939 (5.54)*	0.14896 (5.40)*
Intercept	27.94560 (28.74)*	
$\bar{R}^2$	0.87	
Log-likelihood	−732.5	
No. of observations	341	341
Indian model		
Income per capita	0.00062 (3.19)*	0.00060 (3.56)*
Urbanization	0.24797 (4.95)*	0.24620 (5.47)*
Intercept	34.35820 (33.67)	
$\bar{R}^2$	0.492	
Log-likelihood	−848.3	
No. of observations	252	252
International model		
Income per capita		0.00030 (2.32)**
Urbanization		0.23437 (4.46)*
Service exports		0.20190 (2.94)*
Intercept		35.44928 (11.36)*
$\bar{R}^2$		0.40
No. of observations		93

Notes: The simple version of the country models without group dummy was estimated and rejected according to a χ^2 test; the estimation results are thus not reported in this table. The numbers in parentheses are the *t*-values. * and ** indicate significance at the level of 1% and 10%, respectively.

significant. This implies that both variables are important factors affecting the development of the service sector among the countries, especially in China and India. In addition, it is found that external demand also has a positive impact on service development among the countries. The coefficient of the W variable (the proportion of women in the total non-farming workforce) is statistically insignificant and hence dropped from the final regression. The findings here are, of course, subject to qualifications due to the limitation of data.

4.3 Growth Outlook

Both the Chinese and Indian economies have entered the phase of rapid growth. The consensus view is that this growth will last for decades (Wilson and Purushothaman, 2003; Li *et al.*, 2006). It is thus anticipated that per capita income in both countries will rise over time and subsequently urbanization will accelerate. These factors imply that the service sector in China and India will expand further. This growth will also be boosted by globalization. From 2006 onwards, due to WTO commitments it is expected that China will allow greater foreign participation in the country's service sector including telecommunications, banking, insurance, etc. (Wong and Liang, 2003b). Economic openness will also create more jobs for accountants, lawyers and other financial specialists (Luo, 2001). Further economic liberalization and deregulation in India will ensure sustained growth, including growth in services. Both China and India will also benefit from the WTO's General Agreement on Trade in Services (GATS).[13] Therefore, growth prospects for services in both countries look bright. In particular, growth in services in the two countries will be associated with the following features.

Service sector growth in China will continue and the manufacturing sector will retain its dominance in the economy. Both sectors will show some gains in terms of GDP and employment shares at the expense of agriculture. One source of forecasts, for example, implies that the GDP shares of the primary, manufacturing and service sectors in 2020 will be 5.0%, 45.8% and 49.2%, respectively, and that the employment shares will be 34.2%, 22.4% and 43.4%, respectively.[14] By then, China's service sector will be bigger than the manufacturing sector. However, China

---

[13] For a detailed discussion of GATS' impacts on service trade, see Li and Hou (2003) on China and Chanda (2002) on India.

[14] The output share estimates are based on official statistics and forecasts by Li *et al.* (2006), who predicted that the GDP shares of the primary, manufacturing and service sectors in 2020 would be 7.1%, 52.5% and 40.4%, respectively. The employment shares are the original forecasts by Li *et al.* (2006).

will still have a long way to go to catch up with the advanced economies in the world. For instance, the service sector in 1997 accounted for 58% of total GDP in Japan, 64% in the US, 53% in Germany and 60% in the UK; while the service employment share in the same year was 62% in Japan, 74% in the US, 62% in Germany and 72% in the UK (see Table 4.3). Currently, the service sector contributes to China's economic growth largely due to a shift in labor from agriculture to services (Qin, 2004). This shift in labor will eventually be replaced by a shift from manufacturing to services.

The current momentum of growth in India's service sector will continue in the near future. However, growth in the manufacturing sector will also be accelerated. This trend is already clearly demonstrated in the latest statistics: during the decade 1994–2003, the manufacturing sector grew at an average annual rate of 6.2%, and then this rate jumped to 8.8% in recent years (2004–2009).[15] The consequence of such growth is that the GDP

Table 4.3   Service Sector Shares in Selected Economies

| | Per Capita GNI (US$, 2003) | Service Shares (%) | | | | | |
| | | GDP | | | Employment | | |
		1997	2003	2009	1997	2004	2009
China	1,100	38	40	42	26	31	34
India	540	48	55	59	25	28	34
Germany	25,270	53	69	69	62	67	73
Japan	34,180	58	68	70	62	67	71
UK	28,320	60	72	75	72	76	83
US	37,870	64	75	77	74	78	82

Notes and sources: Chinese and Indian data are drawn from Table A2.2 in the Appendix to Chapter 2. The 2004 employment shares for Germany, Japan, the UK and the US are from the OECD (2005). Other statistics are drawn from Ono (2001), World Bank (2005) and OECD (2010a, 2010b). GNI represents gross national income.

---

[15] These growth rates are estimated using data from the RBI (2009).

shares of both the manufacturing sector and the service sector will expand at the cost of agriculture. For example, the GDP share of services reached 59.3% by the end of the 2008/2009 financial year. The dilemma for India at present is that services account for more than half of GDP but employ just about one third of the country's total workforce (Table 4.3). These shares should match each other, according to the experience of developed economies. A study of the Pacific Basin countries also shows that, without the concomitant progress of industrialization, growth in services in terms of both output and employment will not be sustainable (Park, 1989). The same argument can be applied to India as well.

4.4 Conclusion

This chapter has reviewed and compared service sector developments in China and India. It is found that the role of services in both economies has been rising, with China starting on a lower base. Growth has been mainly driven by increasing specialization of production, rising standards of living and accelerated urbanization in both societies. India's service sector is now the dominant contributor to GDP growth, but employment absorption is not very high in this sector. India's service sector will continue to grow; however, India needs industrialization even more as millions of rural workers have to be employed. In comparison with India, China's service sector is lagging behind. Even from an international perspective, China's service sector is below the average. It can be anticipated that services will expand further as Chinese companies outsource their communications, legal and accounting services and as urbanization accelerates in the coming decades.

Chapter 5

Changing Bilateral Trade

The objective of this chapter is to examine the trends in bilateral trade between China and India in recent years, and to draw possible implications for future trade and economic cooperation between the two nations. This chapter thus adds to the growing literature on the comparison of the Chinese and Indian economies. The rest of the chapter begins with a brief overview of trade affairs in the two economies in Section 5.1. This is followed by an analysis of the major trends in bilateral trade between China and India in Section 5.2. Subsequently, issues related to comparative advantages of the two economies are explored in Section 5.3. Finally, a summary and concluding remarks are presented in Section 5.4.

5.1 Background

A common feature associated with recent growth in China and India is the adoption of pro-trade policies in both countries. The result is that both economies have achieved impressive growth in international trade in the past decade. In fact, the pattern of growth in trade is surprisingly similar in the two countries according to Figure 5.1. During 1993–2009, the total value of trade in China and India grew on average by 17.2% and 15.4% per annum, respectively. Although economic reform in India began about a decade later than in China, India has shown rapid catch-up. The total value of India's trade of about US$465 billion during the 2009/2010 financial year approached

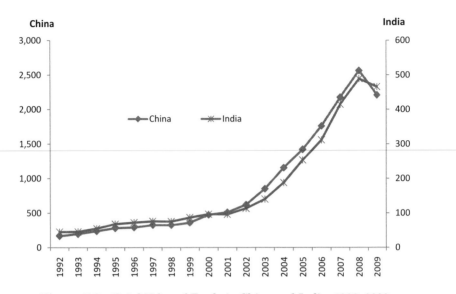

Figure 5.1   Total Value of Trade in China and India, 1992–2009

Notes: The value of trade is expressed in billions of US dollars.
Sources: NBS (2010) and RBI (2010).

China's trade volume of US$474 billion in 2000 (Figure 5.1). This pattern is also reflected in the degree of openness in the two economies: India's openness — defined as the ratio of total trade value over GDP — has maintained a gap with China's since 1992, but this gap has narrowed down in recent years (Figure 5.2).

China is now the world's largest merchandise trader with total trade value amounting to US$2,207 billion in 2009, even though total trade dropped by 13.9% in 2009 due to the global financial crisis. China's export and import activities affect world price movements in many industries. It is anticipated that Indian exports will have the same impact on world commodity trade if the current growth momentum is maintained. Thus, trade developments in and between the two developing giants may have important implications for the world economy, and a thorough understanding of these developments is warranted.

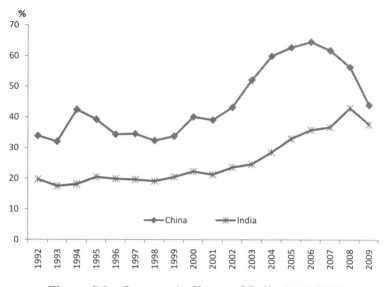

Figure 5.2   Openness in China and India, 1992–2009

Sources: NBS (2010) and RBI (2010).

5.2 China–India Bilateral Trade

Associated with economic reform and rapid growth is the increasing trade and economic cooperation between the two countries. This has been particularly evident since the 1990s, when many Indian entrepreneurs viewed the huge and growing Chinese market as a commercial opportunity while at the same time Chinese companies like Huawei saw the advantages of lower labor costs and a well-developed IT sector in India (*The Economist*, 2005). As a result, bilateral trade between China and India has increased dramatically in the past decade, rising from about US$134 million in 1986 to about US$2 billion in 1997 and about US$34 billion in 2007 (Figure 5.3).[1] As shown in Figure 5.3, China is

---

[1] These numbers are estimated using data from the United Nations Comtrade database SITC Revision 3 (http://unstats.un.org/unsd/comtrade).

US$ billion

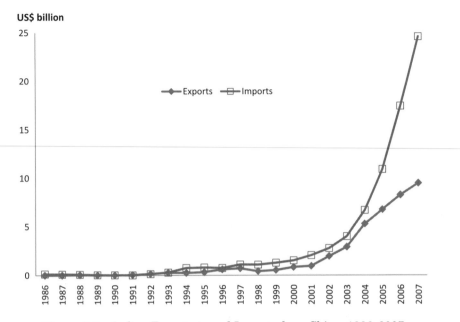

Figure 5.3   Indian Exports to and Imports from China, 1986–2007

Source: Data are extracted from the United Nations Comtrade database SITC Revision 3 (http://unstats.un.org/unsd/comtrade).

currently enjoying a current account surplus against trade with India. This surplus has risen in recent years. China has been the second largest market for Indian exports since 2003.[2] During the 2008/2009 financial year, China was India's second largest trading partner while India was China's 10th largest trading partner (Table 5.1).[3] To gain more insight into this growth in bilateral trade between the two countries, the following subsections will in turn investigate the composition of trade, trade intensity and intra-industry trade.

---

[2] According to the Asian Development Bank's *Key Indicators* (ADB, 2004, 2005), available online (http://www.adb.org/statistics).

[3] These rankings are according to Indian and Chinese trade statistics, respectively (RBI, 2010; NBS, 2010).

Table 5.1 Top Trading Partners of China and India

Ranking	China's Top 10 (US$ billion)	India's Top 10 (US$ billion)
1	334 (US)	47 (UAE)
2	267 (Japan)	41 (China)
3	204 (Hong Kong)	39 (US)
4	186 (South Korea)	25 (Saudi Arabia)
5	129 (Taiwan)	18 (Germany)
6	115 (Germany)	16 (Singapore)
7	60 (Australia)	15 (Iran)
8	57 (Russia)	13 (Hong Kong)
9	54 (Malaysia)	13 (South Korea)
10	52 (India)	12 (UK)

Notes: Author's own compilation. The numbers in the second and third columns are total trade values in billions of US dollars in 2009 for China and during the 2008/2009 financial year for India, respectively.
Sources: NBS (2010) and RBI (2010).

5.2.1 *Composition of Trade*

According to the Standard International Trade Classification (SITC) Revision 3 system, trade in four commodity groups has dominated bilateral trade between China and India (Table 5.2). These groups are SITC 2 (crude materials, inedible, except fuels), SITC 5 (chemicals and related products, n.e.s.), SITC 6 (manufactured goods classified chiefly by material) and SITC 7 (machinery and transport equipment). These groups together accounted for 84.3% of China's exports to India and 96.2% of China's imports from India in 2003.[4]

The statistics in Table 5.2 also show considerable change in the pattern of bilateral trade between the two countries in the past decade. Trade in crude materials (SITC 2) used to have the largest share, amounting to 37.18% of China's exports to India and 61.73% of China's imports from India in 1992. By 2003, however, these shares had shrunk substantially. Instead, trade in manufactured

---

[4] It is noted that there are minor discrepancies if statistics reported by India are used.

goods and transport equipment has become more important, though China's imports of Indian crude materials still have the largest share (especially in recent years), according to Table 5.2.

5.2.2 *Intensity of Trade*

Several statistical indices can be used to measure trade between the two nations. One such index is the trade intensity index (Brown, 1949; Kojima, 1964), which appears in two forms: the export intensity index (XII) and import intensity index (MII). They can be defined as follows:

$$XII_i = \frac{x_{ij} / X_{iw}}{M_{jw} / (M_w - M_{iw})} \tag{5.1}$$

and

$$MII_i = \frac{m_{ij} / M_{iw}}{X_{jw} / (X_w - X_{iw})}, \tag{5.2}$$

where

XII_i = country i's export intensity index
MII_i = country i's import intensity index
x_{ij} = country i's exports to country j
X_{iw} = country i's total exports to the world
M_{jw} = country j's total imports from the world
M_w = world total imports
M_{iw} = country i's total imports from the world
m_{ij} = country i's imports from country j
X_{jw} = country j's total exports to the world
X_w = world total exports
i, j = China and India.

Export and import intensity indices reflect the ratio of the share of country i's trade with country j relative to the share of world trade destined for country j. An index of greater (less) than unity is interpreted as an indication of larger (smaller)-than-expected trade

Table 5.2 China–India Trade Shares by Commodity in Selected Years

SITC Code	Description	Exports to India (%)				Imports from India (%)			
		1992	1997	2003	2007	1992	1997	2003	2007
0	Food and live animals	3.17	1.09	1.40	0.43	9.62	24.24	1.41	1.81
1	Beverages and tobacco	0	0	0.01	0.01	0.86	0	0	0
2	Crude materials, inedible, except fuels	37.20	8.98	5.93	1.59	61.70	38.07	40.11	70.37
3	Mineral fuels, lubricants and related materials	11.20	18.87	7.05	1.27	2.14	2.89	0.39	0.22
4	Animal and vegetable oils, fats and waxes	0.18	0.06	0.02	0.01	0.18	1.97	0.37	0.58
5	Chemicals and related products, n.e.s.	27.50	33.53	26.15	18.19	6.04	5.85	15.59	9.07
6	Manufactured goods classified chiefly by material	10.60	15.16	23.57	24.73	17.40	24.25	36.74	12.67
7	Machinery and transport equipment	6.94	17.58	28.65	49.10	0.91	1.30	3.80	3.81
8	Miscellaneous manufactured articles	3.16	4.74	7.21	4.59	0.90	1.42	1.36	1.24
9	Not classified elsewhere	0	0	0.01	0.08	0.23	0	0.22	0.24
	Total	100	100	100	100	100	100	100	100

Source: The statistics are derived using data from the UN Comtrade database SITC Revision 3 (http://unstats.un.org/unsd/comtrade) and based on China's reported export and import values.

Table 5.3   Intensity of Trade Between China and India

Trade Intensity	1992	1997	2003	2007
Export				
China to India	0.291	0.678	0.715	1.125
India to China	0.366	0.812	0.849	0.899
Import				
China from India	0.400	0.970	1.146	1.250
India from China	0.255	0.807	0.874	1.200

Note and source: Author's own estimates using data from the UN Comtrade database SITC Revision 3 (http://unstats.un.org/unsd/comtrade).

flow between the two parties concerned. Table 5.3 demonstrates that by 2003 all export and import intensity indices with one exception were smaller than unity, implying that China and India were trading less than they should. This situation has, however, changed recently. By 2007, three of the four trade intensity figures were greater than unity according to Table 5.3. Thus, bilateral trade between the two countries increased substantially between 2003 and 2007, though the estimates in Table 5.3 imply that India could export more to China than its current level.

5.2.3 *Intra-Industry Trade*

Another important feature associated with trade is the dramatic increase in intra-industry trade (IIT). To provide an assessment, the following conventional IIT index proposed by Grubel and Lloyd (1975) is computed:

$$IIT_{ic} = \frac{x_{ic} + m_{ic} - |x_{ic} - m_{ic}|}{x_{ic} + m_{ic}}, \qquad (5.3)$$

where

IIT_{ic} = index of intra-industry trade in commodity group c for country i

x_{ic} = value of exports of commodity group c by country i

m_{ic} = value of imports of commodity group c by country i.

The IIT index defined in Equation (5.3) has a value range between zero and one, or between zero and 100 in percentage form.[5] A large value implies greater trade between firms in the same industry. Table 5.4 demonstrates that most intra-industry trade (with an IIT index greater than 0.5) has occurred in the commodity groups of SITCs 5, 6 and 7 at the two-digit level. Five other groups — SITCs 23, 29, 33, 84 and 89 — also recorded high IIT scores calculated using 2003 trade statistics. In 2007, there were some changes in the IIT scores but most groups with high IIT scores in 2003 still had high scores.

5.3 Are China and India Competitors?

To compare the competitiveness of each country in the trade of a particular commodity group, the revealed comparative advantage (RCA) index is often computed using the following formula:

$$RCA_{ic} = \frac{x_{ic} / X_{iw}}{x_{cw} / X_w}, \tag{5.4}$$

where

RCA_{ic} = revealed comparative advantage index of commodity group c for country i
x_{ic} = value of exports of commodity group c by country i
X_{iw} = value of total exports by country i
x_{cw} = value of world exports of commodity group c
X_w = value of total world exports.

Country i has a comparative advantage in exporting commodity group c when RCA_{ic} has a value greater than unity, that is, when country i's export share of commodity group c is larger than the world export share of the same commodity

---

[5] It is noted that alternative forms of the IIT index have been proposed by Hamilton and Kniest (1991), Greenaway *et al.* (1994) and Brulhart (1994).

Table 5.4   Intra-Industry Trade Indices

SITC Code	Description	2003	2007
84	Articles of apparel and clothing accessories	0.908	0.306
53	Dyeing, tanning and coloring materials	0.888	0.784
78	Road vehicles (including air-cushion vehicles)	0.843	0.074
29	Crude animal and vegetable materials, n.e.s.	0.838	0.945
68	Non-ferrous metals	0.807	0.899
33	Petroleum, petroleum products	0.739	0.580
55	Essential oils and resinoids and perfume materials	0.716	0.673
74	General industrial machinery and machine parts, n.e.s.	0.703	0.242
89	Miscellaneous manufactured articles, n.e.s.	0.697	0.517
51	Organic chemicals	0.694	0.611
58	Plastics in non-primary forms	0.586	0.179
73	Metalworking machinery	0.580	0.066
66	Non-metallic mineral manufactures, n.e.s.	0.545	0.983
23	Crude rubber (including synthetic and reclaimed)	0.519	0.838
71	Power-generating machinery and equipment	0.508	0.113
77	Electrical machinery and appliances, n.e.s., and electrical parts	0.506	0.166
05	Vegetables and fruit	0.472	0.669
62	Rubber manufactures, n.e.s.	0.466	0.076
59	Chemical materials and products, n.e.s.	0.456	0.534
65	Textile yarn, fabrics, made-up articles, and related products	0.440	0.210
54	Medicinal and pharmaceutical products	0.438	0.153
27	Crude fertilizers and crude minerals	0.394	0.222
72	Machinery specialized for particular industries	0.349	0.077
64	Paper, paperboard and articles of paper pulp	0.332	0.088
26	Textile fibers	0.323	0.457

Note: IIT indices are based on the values of China's exports to India and China's imports from India.

group.[6] On the contrary, if RCA_{ic} is less than unity, country i has a comparative disadvantage.

According to Table 5.5, China has shown a comparative advantage mainly in manufactured goods (SITCs 6 and 8) and machinery and transport equipment (SITC 7). The same table also reveals that Indian comparative advantage lies in commodity groups SITCs 0, 2, 5, 6 and 8. Apparently, both China and India have shown a comparative advantage in manufactured goods (SITCs 6

Table 5.5 Comparative Advantage Indices

SITC Code	Description	China			India		
		1997	**2003**	**2007**	**1997**	**2003**	**2007**
0	Food and live animals	0.904	0.696	0.487	2.334	1.726	1.568
1	Beverages and tobacco	0.576	0.254	0.145	0.858	0.449	0.438
2	Crude materials, inedible, except fuels	0.551	0.339	0.338	1.229	1.455	3.373
3	Mineral fuels, lubricants and related materials	0.446	0.247	0.137	0.132	0.570	1.354
4	Animal and vegetable oils, fats and waxes	0.777	0.064	0.056	1.118	0.933	0.666
5	Chemicals and related products, n.e.s.	0.583	0.405	0.454	1.024	1.056	1.028
6	Manufactured goods classified chiefly by material	1.266	1.176	1.216	2.540	2.749	1.990
7	Machinery and transport equipment	0.619	1.092	1.246	0.208	0.248	0.297
8	Miscellaneous manufactured articles	2.950	2.225	2.166	1.467	1.488	1.277
9	Not classified elsewhere	0.065	0.081	0.041	0.673	0.406	0.267

Note and source: Author's own estimates using data from the UN Comtrade database SITC Revision 3 (http://unstats.un.org/unsd/comtrade).

---

[6] It should be pointed out that this RCA index is asymmetric in the sense that it ranges from one to infinity for products in which a country has a comparative advantage, but only from zero to one for the case of comparative disadvantage. To correct this skewed distribution, several symmetric RCA indices have been proposed (e.g. Dalum *et al.*, 1998; Laursen, 1998).

and 8). There must be some competition in these areas. However, this conclusion is based on calculations at a highly aggregate level. At a more disaggregate level, the two countries may have a comparative advantage in different commodity groups as shown by Balasubramanyam and Wei (2005a). In addition, the intra-industry trade indices presented in Table 5.4 show that there may be more IIT in commodities in which both countries have a comparative advantage (e.g. SITCs 66, 68, 84 and 89). Finally, Table 5.5 also demonstrates that there are areas where there is no overlap in the two countries' comparative advantage and thus the two countries do not compete with each other. These areas include SITCs 0, 2, 5 and 7, according to Table 5.5.

5.4 Summary and Concluding Remarks

To sum up, China and India have enjoyed unprecedented economic growth in the past decade. This growth has substantially lifted the status of the two countries in the world economy. Associated with this growth is the rapid expansion in bilateral trade between the two largest developing economies. It is reported that the total volume of bilateral trade between China and India in 2009 reached US$43 billion, making India the ninth largest trader of China.[7] As economic reforms deepen in the two economies, high economic growth is expected to be sustained for some time. This growth will in turn generate more trade between the two neighboring economies.

Further increase in bilateral trade is also determined by several other factors. First, the estimated trade intensity indices in this chapter have shown that China and India are not trading at a level as high as it should be. Thus, there is potential for growth in bilateral trade between the two economies. Chinese and Indian policy makers are now working together to improve trade and economic cooperation. Diplomatic relations between the two countries are better now than at any time since the 1960s (*The Economist*, 2005). In particular, since Atal Bihari Vajpayee, the then-Prime

---

[7] This is based on Chinese official statistics (NBS, 2010).

Table 5.6 Structure of the Chinese and Indian Economies (% of GDP)

	China			India		
	Primary	**Industry**	**Services**	**Primary**	**Industry**	**Services**
1986	27.1	44.0	28.9	33.4	22.7	43.9
1995	19.8	47.2	33.0	29.5	23.3	47.1
2004	13.1	46.2	40.8	20.2	23.9	55.8
2009	10.6	46.8	42.6	17.0	23.8	59.3

Notes and sources: All data are drawn from the ADB (2005), NBS (2010) and RBI (2010).

Minister of India, visited China in June 2003, the two countries have reduced tariffs on each other's export products considerably.

Second, growth in bilateral trade is also possible if each country exploits its own comparative advantage. There is an overlap in both countries' comparative advantage in some commodities, according to the estimates in this chapter. However, the two countries can still expand trade in areas where there is no overlap in their comparative advantage. There is also scope for an increase in intra-industry trade in some areas where the two are competing with each other.

Third, the two economies complement each other in some areas. While China has a dominant industrial sector in the economy, India has a strong service sector (Table 5.6). Therefore, the two countries can offer each other valuable experience and lessons. China can learn from India to develop a strong service sector. India has to expand its manufacturing sector and specifically improve the sector's competitiveness. In terms of manufacturing development, China may offer a model for India to follow.

Finally, the existing practice has shown that bilateral free trade agreements (FTAs) offer a second-best solution to world free trade. Research findings demonstrate that FTAs have boosted bilateral trade between partners (Wu, 2006). In particular, neighboring economies could potentially benefit more from an FTA. China and India should explore the possibility of signing a free trade agreement sooner rather than later.

Chapter 6

▬▬▬▬

Energy Consumption and Carbon Emission

As the economies of China and India take off, global concerns about their impact on energy consumption and climate change have increased and hence led to an expansion of the literature.[1] This chapter presents a comparative perspective of energy and carbon emission intensities across the world economies. The findings are then employed to draw implications for energy consumption and CO_2 emission in Asia, especially in the emerging giants of China and India. The rest of this chapter starts with a cross-country comparison of energy consumption and CO_2 emission in Section 6.1. This is followed by a discussion of energy and CO_2 emission intensities across the countries in Section 6.2, whereby the sources of cross-country variations are investigated. The findings are subsequently employed to gain insights into energy consumption and CO_2 emission in Asia including the two giants, China and India (Section 6.3). The final section (Section 6.4) concludes the chapter.

---

[1] For example, Shalizi (2007) presents some preliminary information about energy and emission intensities in China and India, and has adopted a multi-regional global model to forecast energy consumption in the two countries up to the year 2050, while the IEA (2007) has delivered a special report on China and India. Other studies include Srivastava (1997), Nag and Parikh (2000), Paul and Bhattacharya (2004a, 2004b), Crompton and Wu (2005), Wu *et al.* (2006), and Zou and Chau (2006).

6.1 Cross-Country Comparison of Energy Consumption and CO_2 Emission

Figure 6.1 (Panel A) shows that in 2006, among 128 countries, the world's largest economy, i.e. the USA, was also the largest energy consumer, followed in turn by China, Russia, India, Japan and Germany.[2] In comparison with the United States, among the major economies, the Japanese economy tends to be the most energy-efficient one; while the Chinese economy is the least energy-efficient economy, followed by India and Russia. However, to some extent, Figure 6.1 may also reflect the possibility of underestimation of the size of the Chinese and Indian economies in terms of US dollars. In fact, if GDP is measured in international (purchasing power parity) currency, India appears to be an "average" country (see Part I of Figure A6.1 in the Appendix to this chapter) and China is slightly above the "average" trend.[3] However, Japan and Russia are definitely the outliers, namely, the most efficient vs. least efficient economies.

In general, energy consumption per capita is positively related to the level of income, that is, GDP per capita (Panel B, Figure 6.1; see also Part II of Figure A6.1 in the Appendix to this chapter). But there are exceptions. Energy-abundant economies such as Bahrain, Kuwait, Iceland, Trinidad and Tobago, Russia, and United Arab Emirates (UAE) tend to be outliers, with an exceptionally high per capita energy consumption relative to their income level. In the meantime, Hong Kong, Denmark, Norway, Switzerland and Japan are at the other extreme with a relatively low per capita consumption of energy. Among the middle-income economies (with per capita income of just over US$10,000 in 2006), Trinidad and Tobago shows an exceptionally high consumption per capita. Among the economies with per capita income under US$5,000, India is once again very

---

[2] Unless stated otherwise, data used in this chapter are drawn from the online World Development Indicators database (http://www.worldbank.org).

[3] It is noticed that the World Bank has revised downwards its estimates of China's GDP in recent years. If the initial GDP estimates are used, China would appear as a perfect "average" country.

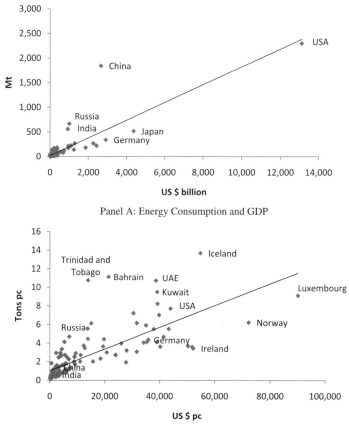

Panel A: Energy Consumption and GDP

Panel B: Per Capita Energy Consumption and GDP

Figure 6.1 Energy Consumption and GDP in Selected Economies, 2006

Notes: Author's own work using statistics from the World Development Indicators online database (http://www.worldbank.org). Mt: million tons; tons pc: tons per capita.

much an "average" country in terms of per capita energy consumption and China is slightly above the trend line (see Part I of Figure A6.2 in the Appendix to this chapter). However, most transitional economies in Eastern Europe tend to be outliers (e.g. Belarus, Bulgaria, Russia, Ukraine and Uzbekistan), implying ample scope for improvement in energy efficiency in these economies.

In terms of total CO_2 emission in 2006, China led the world economies with the US being right behind as the number two

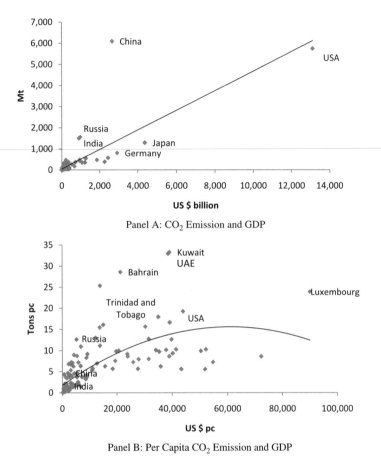

Panel A: CO_2 Emission and GDP

Panel B: Per Capita CO_2 Emission and GDP

Figure 6.2 CO_2 Emission and GDP in Selected Economies, 2006

Notes: Author's own work using statistics from the World Development Indicators online database (http://www.worldbank.org). Mt: million tons; tons pc: tons per capita.

emitter, followed in turn by Russia, India, Japan and Germany (Panel A, Figure 6.2). This situation is consistent with the consumption pattern of energy (Panel A, Figure 6.1) except that China and the US have switched positions. Once again, among the largest economies besides the US, China, India and Russia, especially China, appear to be more emission-intensive, while Japan and Germany are less emission-intensive. This is still true for

China and Russia even if GDP is measured in international currency (see Part I of Figure A6.3 in the Appendix to this chapter).

On a per capita basis, however, the situation is quite different. Figure 6.2 (Panel B) shows the distribution of CO_2 emission per capita against income level. Apparently, oil-rich economies such as Bahrain, Kuwait, Trinidad and Tobago, and UAE are outliers. So are the four developed economies, namely, Australia, Canada, the United States and Luxembourg. Figure 6.2 also clearly demonstrates an inverted U-curve and thus confirms the existence of the environmental Kuznets curve (EKC) as argued by others (Grossman and Krueger, 1995; Selden and Song, 1994). If the five outliers with the largest emission per capita (Bahrain, Kuwait, Luxembourg, Trinidad and Tobago, and UAE) are removed, the inverted-U relationship implies a turning point at US$36,000 per capita. This relationship is still correct and the turning point is at a similar income level (approximately PPP$41,700 per capita in 2006) if an international benchmarking income is used (see Part II of Figure A6.3 in the Appendix to this chapter).

As shown, most less developed countries (LDCs) fall into the left half of the inverted U-curve in Figure 6.2 (Panel B). In consistency with their energy inefficiency, several former centrally planned economies tend to be outliers (such as Russia, Estonia and Kazakhstan). As for the two Asian giants, India is slightly above the "average" trend in the world while China's position is much higher than the world average (see Part II of Figure A6.2 in the Appendix to this chapter). In addition, there is a close relationship between CO_2 emission and energy consumption among countries in the world in terms of either aggregate or per capita amount (Figure 6.3). For the latter, however, four countries tend to be outliers that consume either extremely clean energy (Iceland) or relatively emission-intensive energy (Bahrain, Kuwait and UAE).[4]

---

[4] In 2005, according to the online database of the International Energy Agency (http://www.iea.org), Iceland's energy supply included 56.0% from geothermal/solar/wind sources, 16.6% from hydro energy, 24.6% from oil and 2.7% from coal.

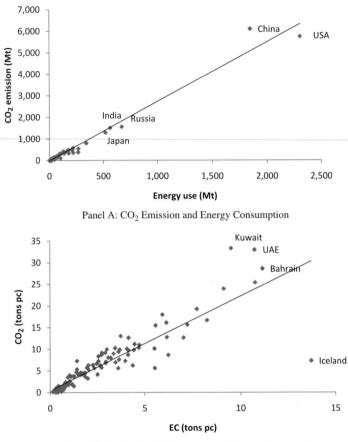

Panel A: CO_2 Emission and Energy Consumption

Panel B: Per Capita CO_2 Emission and Energy Consumption

Figure 6.3 CO_2 Emission and Energy Consumption in Selected Economies, 2006

Notes: Author's own work using statistics from the World Development Indicators online database (http://www.worldbank.org). Mt: million tons; tons pc: tons per capita.

6.2 Energy and Carbon Emission Intensities

Energy intensity (EI) or carbon emission intensity (CI) is formally defined as the amount of energy consumed or CO_2 emitted per unit of GDP. In general, energy and carbon emission intensities decline as income increases (see Figure A6.4 in the Appendix to this chapter). There is, however, no clear evidence of the existence of an environmental Kuznets curve. In terms of international dollars, carbon emission intensity and income level tend to follow an inverted U-curve and hence confirm the existence of the environmental Kuznets curve with a turning point of PPP$14,300 per head (see Part II of Figure A6.5 in the Appendix to this chapter). But this does not apply to the relationship between energy intensity and per capita income (see Part I of Figure A6.5 in the Appendix to this chapter).

Energy and carbon emission intensities may also be affected by other factors such as the level of urbanization and industrialization, and development of the service sector. To examine the impact of these factors on cross-country variations in energy and carbon emission intensities, a regression analysis approach is employed. Given the availability of data, several factors are considered in the analysis. These include the stage of economic development, economic structure (service and manufacturing sector income shares), and level of urbanization. It must be pointed out that energy and carbon emission intensities are also likely to be affected by energy prices and environmental regulations. The latter are, however, excluded from the regression analysis due to the paucity of data.

The stage of economic development variable (Y) together with its quadratic form is included to check whether an environmental Kuznets curve is observed and, if so, where the turning point is. It is measured by GDP per capita and expressed in terms of US dollars. Both energy (EI) and carbon emission (CI) intensities are also affected by manufacturing activities or the level of industrialization (IND) among the economies. The degree of urbanization (URB) and service sector development (SER) can be closely related, but may have different impacts on energy and emission intensities. Symbolically,

$$\log Intensity = \alpha_0 + \alpha_1 \log Y + \alpha_2 (\log Y)^2 + \alpha_3 IND \\ + \alpha_4 SER + \alpha_5 URB + u, \tag{6.1}$$

where *intensity* represents both energy (EI) and carbon emission (CI) intensities.

Table 6.1   Estimation Results

Variables	log EI		log CI	
Constant	2.194 (9.60)[a]	3.368 (2.97)[a]	0.892 (2.19)[b]	−5.234 (−3.085)
log Y	−0.291 (−7.45)[a]	−0.586 (−2.08)[b]	−0.131 (−1.89)[c]	1.588 (3.508)
$(\log Y)^2$		0.017 (1.06)		−0.108 (−3.958)
IND	0.008 (1.48)	0.010 (1.71)[c]	0.022 (2.24)[b]	0.021 (2.203)
SER	−0.013 (−4.30)[a]	−0.014 (−4.41)[a]	−0.012 (−2.24)[b]	−0.012 (−1.868)
URB	−0.005 (−1.95)[c]	−0.004 (−1.56)	−0.000 (−0.04)	−0.002 (−0.42)
Adjusted R^2	0.74	0.74	0.17	
Sample size	105	105	105	

Notes: a, b and c indicate significance at the level of 1%, 5% and 10%, respectively. The results are based on 2006 data with several outliers being removed.

In general, the regression results in Table 6.1 show that both energy and carbon emission intensities are positively affected by the level of industrialization and negatively affected by the degree of urbanization and the development of services. It can be concluded that energy intensity has a U-shaped relationship with income, while emission intensity follows an inverted U-shaped curve. Thus, the environmental Kuznets relationship is once again confirmed in this cross-country analysis. Controlling for other factors, emission intensity declines when economic development reaches a certain level, that is, the turning point. For developed economies, a reduction in emission intensity will result from the combined forces of service expansion and manufacturing contraction. On the other hand, for low-income economies, the direction of change is not clear as many countries have yet to develop their manufacturing sectors and to expand their services and urban sectors. Growth in the former will become a force for the further rise of emission intensity, while expansion in the latter will imply a potential fall in emission intensity.

6.3 Where Are China and India Heading?

While the regression results reported in the preceding section indicate the potential sources of variation in energy and carbon emission intensities, it is difficult to draw implications for individual economies given the diversity of economic structures, energy consumption patterns and resource endowments among the world economies. This section sheds some light on the future trend of energy consumption and carbon emission in China and India by comparing the two Asian giants with the world's major economies. All together these economies are here called the group-26.[5]

On a per capita basis, the trend of changes in energy consumption and carbon emission is not unambiguous. In general, the world's major economies are divided into different models or clubs, ranging from less energy/emission-intensive economies (such as Portugal, Hong Kong, Denmark, France and Sweden) to more energy/emission-intensive ones (such as Russia, Luxembourg, Canada, Australia and the US). These distinctions are clearly illustrated in Figure A6.6 in the Appendix to this chapter. Whichever club that China and India will eventually join has important implications for the world's energy consumption and carbon emission. Should China and India opt for the energy/emission-intensive model, per capita energy consumption and carbon emission would be much higher than those under the cleaner development model pursued by countries such as Japan, France, Sweden and Portugal (see Table 6.2). Such a scenario would put enormous pressure on the world's environment and resources, given the fact that China and India together account for about one-third of the world population.

Among the world's major economies, energy and carbon emission intensities fall as per capita income increases (Figure 6.4). It can be anticipated that China and India will follow this trend. Both energy and carbon emission intensities in the two giants will decline over time. This is confirmed by historical statistics

---

[5] These economies include 21 OECD members (Australia, Austria, Belgium, Canada, Denmark, Finland, France, Germany, Hong Kong, Japan, Korea, Luxembourg, the Netherlands, New Zealand, Norway, Portugal, Singapore, Spain, Sweden, the United Kingdom and the United States), four East Asian economies (Indonesia, Malaysia, the Philippines and Thailand) and Russia.

Table 6.2   Summary Statistics of Selected Economies

Countries	GDPpc	ECpc	CEpc	EI	CI
India	824	0.505	1.360	0.613	1.650
China	2,027	1.408	4.652	0.694	2.295
Japan	34,148	4.057	10.117	0.119	0.296
Sweden	43,297	5.528	5.599	0.128	0.129
Denmark	50,367	3.693	9.914	0.073	0.197
Submean	42,604	4.426	8.543	0.107	0.207
Australia	34,997	5.924	17.960	0.169	0.513
United States	43,962	7.718	19.265	0.176	0.438
Luxembourg	90,039	9.115	23.916	0.101	0.266
Submean	56,332	7.586	20.381	0.149	0.406

Notes: GDPpc, ECpc and CEpc refer to per capita GDP (US$), energy consumption (tons) and carbon emission (tons), respectively, in 2006. EI and CI represent energy intensity (kg/US$) and carbon emission intensity (kg/US$), respectively.
Source: Author's own calculation using statistics from the World Development Indicators online database (http://www.worldbank.org).

from China and India (Figure 6.5). In particular, the fall in energy and emission intensities has been impressive in China, though both intensities were very volatile in the 1970s and 1980s. In comparison with China, the changes have been less dramatic in India, which had much lower energy and emission intensities in 1971 than China, reflecting the relatively minor share of the manufacturing sector in the Indian economy. Both energy and carbon emission intensities in India declined in the 1970s, but remained relatively stable in the 1980s and 1990s. During the decades leading to 2006, both energy and emission intensities converged in the two economies.

If the four largest Asian economies (China, Japan, India and South Korea) are considered together with the world's largest economy (the US), an interesting finding is that they are converging in terms of both energy intensity and carbon emission intensity (Figure 6.6).[6] In particular, energy intensity has

---

[6] China, India, Japan, South Korea and the US together may be called the group-5.

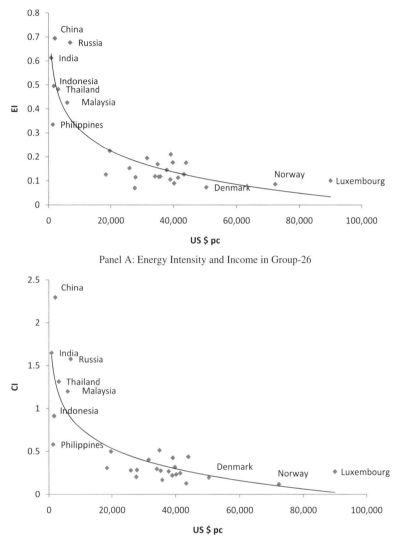

Panel A: Energy Intensity and Income in Group-26

Panel B: Carbon Emission Intensity and Income in Group-26

Figure 6.4 Energy Intensity, Carbon Emission Intensity and Income in Group-26

Notes: EI: energy intensity (kg/US$); US$ pc: US dollars per capita; CI: carbon emission intensity (kg/US$).

Source: Author's own calculation using 2006 statistics from the World Development Indicators online database (http://www.worldbank.org).

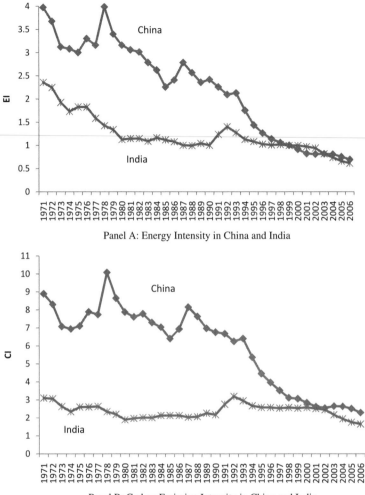

Panel A: Energy Intensity in China and India

Panel B: Carbon Emission Intensity in China and India

Figure 6.5   Energy Intensity and Carbon Emission Intensity in China and India

Notes: EI: energy intensity (kg/US$); CI: carbon emission intensity (kg/US$).
Source: Author's own calculation using statistics from the World Development Indicators online database (http://www.worldbank.org).

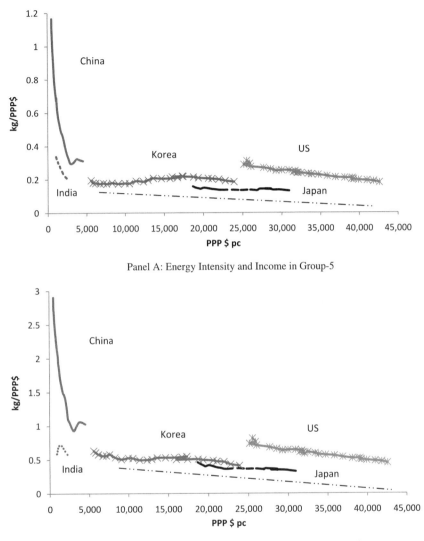

Panel A: Energy Intensity and Income in Group-5

Panel B: Carbon Emission Intensity and Income in Group-5

Figure 6.6 Energy Intensity, Carbon Emission Intensity and Income in Group-5

Notes: The *x*-axis and *y*-axis represent per capita GDP (PPP$) and energy or carbon emission intensity (kg/PPP$), respectively, covering the period 1980–2006.

Source: Author's own calculation using statistics from the World Development Indicators online database (http://www.worldbank.org).

declined dramatically in both China and India. By 2006, in terms of energy and emission intensities, India reached a similar level as South Korea in the 1970s. In China, both energy and carbon emission intensities have declined continuously over time. The intensities bottomed in 2002 and since then the trend of decline has stalled and even reversed in some years (Figure 6.6).[7] The sharp contrast between the US and the four Asian giants raises the question of whether there is an Asian model in energy use and emission control.

Given the fact that the four largest economies in Asia are at different stages of development, will China and India be able to tunnel through the South Korea and Japan path? That is, will China and India be able to perform even better than South Korea and Japan in the future (following the dash-dot-dot lines in Figure 6.6)? If China and India can maintain their practices in the past decades, tunneling through is highly possible as there is still a long way to go for the two countries to catch up with their rich Asian neighbors.

6.4 Concluding Remarks

In summary, there is clear evidence of the close association between income and energy consumption and hence CO_2 emission. As expected, the world's biggest economies are also the largest energy consumers as well as carbon emitters. On a per capita basis, however, there is considerable variation among the nations in terms of energy consumption and carbon emission. The major economies in the world are divided into different clubs, from less energy/emission-intensive to more energy/emission-intensive. Whether China and India will join the energy/emission-intensive

---

[7] It is noticed that the use of PPP-measured income is controversial. The World Bank has revised China's PPP-based income statistics in recent years. Thus, the turnaround of energy and carbon emission intensities in recent years might be due to data inaccuracy.

group or not has important implications for the world's energy supply and hence control of climate changes.

There is already evidence that energy and carbon emission intensities have fallen substantially in the two giants, particularly in China. From a comparative perspective, the four largest Asian economies — China, Japan, India and South Korea — are also converging in terms of energy and emission intensities. Asian countries have shown a unique Asian model in energy use and emission controls. Given the current development stage and long catch-up process of China and India, the two countries have a good chance to "tunnel through" — that is, to pursue an even less energy- and emission-intensive strategy than South Korea and Japan, which are already champions in terms of energy efficiency and emission control among the developed world.

Appendix

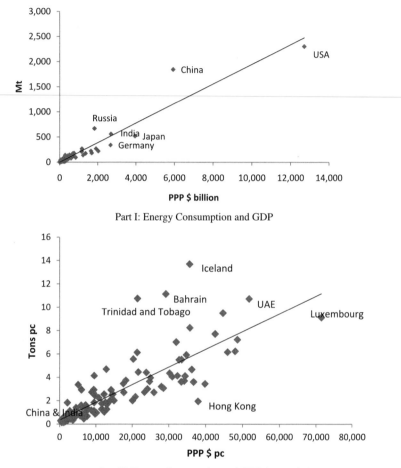

Part I: Energy Consumption and GDP

Part II: Energy Consumption and GDP (per capita)

Figure A6.1   Energy Consumption and Income (PPP-based) in Selected Economies, 2006

Notes: Author's own work using statistics from the World Development Indicators online database (http://www.worldbank.org). Mt: million tons; tons pc: tons per capita.

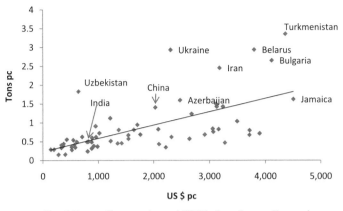

Part I: Energy Consumption and GDP in Low-Income Economies

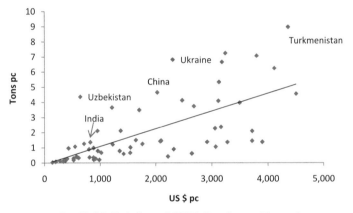

Part II: CO_2 Emission and GDP in Low-Income Economies

Figure A6.2 Energy Consumption, CO_2 Emission and GDP in Selected Economies, 2006

Notes: Author's own work using statistics from the World Development Indicators online database (http://www.worldbank.org). Tons pc: tons per capita; US$ pc: US dollars per capita.

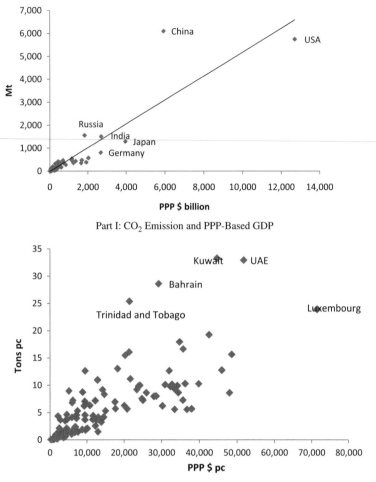

Part I: CO$_2$ Emission and PPP-Based GDP

Part II: CO$_2$ Emission and PPP-Based GDP (per capita)

Figure A6.3   CO$_2$ Emission and Income (PPP-based) in Selected Economies, 2006

Notes: Author's own work using statistics from the World Development Indicators online database (http://www.worldbank.org). Mt: million tons; tons pc: tons per capita; PPP\$ pc: purchasing power parity dollars per capita.

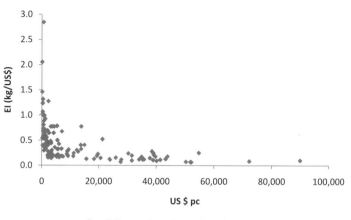

Part I: Energy Intensity and Per Capita Income

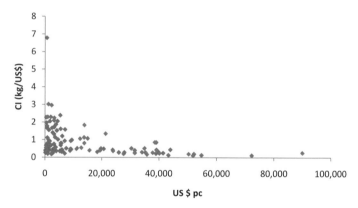

Part II: Carbon Emission Intensity and Per Capita Income

Figure A6.4   Energy Intensity, Carbon Emission Intensity and Income, 2006

Notes: Author's own work using statistics from the World Development Indicators online database (http://www.worldbank.org). EI and CI refer to energy intensity and carbon emission intensity, respectively, and are expressed in kilograms per US dollar. The *x*-axis represents per capita income (US dollars per capita).

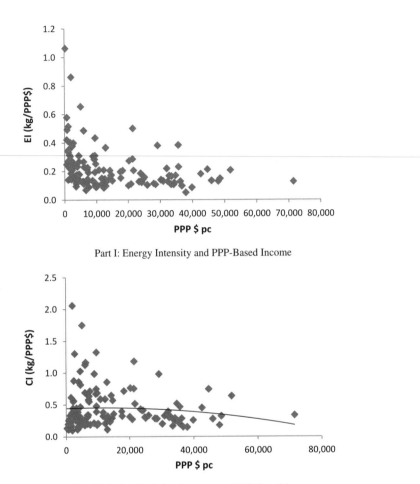

Part I: Energy Intensity and PPP-Based Income

Part II: Carbon Emission Intensity and PPP-Based Income

Figure A6.5   Energy Intensity, Carbon Emission Intensity and PPP-Based Income, 2006

Notes: Author's own work using statistics from the World Development Indicators online database (http://www.worldbank.org). EI and CI refer to energy intensity and carbon emission intensity, respectively, and are expressed in kilograms per purchasing power parity dollar. The *x*-axis represents per capita income (PPP dollars per capita).

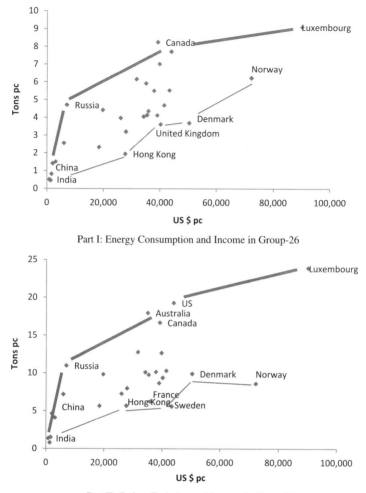

Part I: Energy Consumption and Income in Group-26

Part II: Carbon Emission and Income in Group-26

Figure A6.6 Energy Consumption, Carbon Emission and Income in Group-26

Notes: Author's own work using 2006 statistics from the World Development Indicators online database (http://www.worldbank.org). The *x*-axis and *y*-axis represent per capita income (US dollars per capita) and tons per capita, respectively.

Chapter 7

Pollution Control and Economic Growth

Comparing recent economic development in China and India has attracted a lot of attention internationally.[1] However, work on this topic would be incomplete without a comparative study of pollution in the two developing giants. With this in mind, the objective of this chapter is to fill the gap in the literature and present a comparative analysis of the current conditions of pollution, especially industrial pollution, in China and India. Section 7.1 highlights some stylized facts about the two nations' current growth and environmental consequences. This is followed by an examination of the sources of pollution in Section 7.2. Subsequently, issues associated with carbon emissions in China and India are briefly discussed in Section 7.3. Section 7.4 sheds some light on the potential actions or policy responses that Chinese and Indian policy makers may undertake in the near future. Finally, the chapter concludes with some summary remarks in Section 7.5.

7.1 High Growth at the Expense of the Environment

Over the last three decades, the world has been astonished by the miraculous economic growth in China and India. For instance, during 1980–2010, the average real rate of GDP growth was 9.8% in China and 5.6% in India (see Figure 2.1). Though there is a

---

[1] Examples of recent literature include Swamy (2003), Srinivasan (2004), Tseng and Cowen (2005), Das (2006) and Winters and Yusuf (2007).

gap in the growth performance between the two countries, India has shown rapid catch-up with China in the past decade, particularly in recent years. With both countries' governments being fully committed to the goal of high economic growth, the current development momentum is expected to continue for decades.

However, high growth has been achieved with severe environmental damages such as deforestation, widespread acid rain and deteriorating ambient air quality. These consequences threaten human living space and health, and are costly to deal with. A government report shows that the environmental cost amounted to 3.05% of China's GDP in 2004.[2] In India, it is estimated that the damage and degradation of natural resources is equivalent to about 10% of the country's GDP (Pachauri, 2004). While these estimates may be debatable, there is no doubt that pollution has serious health and economic consequences.

One of the most notorious consequences is air pollution, which has reached an unprecedented level and is deteriorating in both countries. Though the measurement of air quality is complicated, there are a few criteria pollutants for which regulators keep a watchful eye through regular monitoring. These are taken as indicators of air quality in a particular region or city. The most watched pollutants include particulate matter (PM), nitrogen dioxide (NO_2), sulfur dioxide (SO_2) and carbon dioxide (CO_2).

Due to pollution, the ambient air quality in major cities in China and India is now very poor. For example, the annual average concentration of suspended particulate matter (PM_{10}) is very high in both Chinese and Indian cities (Table 7.1).[3] Indeed, many cities have exceeded the officially designated critical levels, not to mention the ambient air quality standards set by the World Health Organization (WHO, 2006). In China, the average concentration of sulfur dioxide and nitrogen dioxide is especially high.

---

[2] This estimated figure was released on the Chinese government official website under the title "Green GDP Accounting Study Report 2004 Issued" (http://www.gov.cn/; September 11, 2006).

[3] PM_{10} is used to describe particles of 10 μm or less in aerodynamic diameter.

Table 7.1 Ambient Air Quality Status (annual average, $\mu g/m^3$)

Chinese Cities	Particulate Matter (PM_{10})	Sulfur Dioxide (SO_2)	Nitrogen Dioxide (NO_2)	Indian Cities	Particulate Matter (PM_{10})	Sulfur Dioxide (SO_2)	Nitrogen Dioxide (NO_2)
Beijing	148	47	66	Kanpur	409	7	21
Urumqi	136	88	67	Delhi	384	9	47
Xi'an	135	53	43	Faridabad	353	9	22
Lanzhou	129	60	42	Patna	298	10	41
Shijiazhuang	128	43	35	Ludhiana	272	12	30
Taiyuan	124	76	27	Dehradun	269	25	28
Wuhan	123	61	55	Raipur	259	12	34
Shenyang	119	54	36	Kolkata	259	10	39
Jinan	118	56	23	Jaipur	239	5	43
Hefei	116	23	26	Mumbai	230	10	23
Xining	115	28	35	Ahmedabad	223	10	21
Chengdu	111	62	49	Guwahati	194	7	20
Chongqing	108	65	44	Chandigarh	189	6	12
Hangzhou	107	60	57	Bangalore	186	9	26
Nanjing	107	58	51	Jammu	182	n.a.	n.a.
Zhengzhou	105	69	45	Indore	176	6	13
Changsha	104	65	41	Chennai	176	7	10
Harbin	102	48	60	Jamshedpur	167	19	30
Changchun	99	30	38	Hyderabad	158	5	22

(Continued)

Table 7.1   (*Continued*)

Chinese Cities	Particulate Matter (PM$_{10}$)	Sulfur Dioxide (SO$_2$)	Nitrogen Dioxide (NO$_2$)	Indian Cities	Particulate Matter (PM$_{10}$)	Sulfur Dioxide (SO$_2$)	Nitrogen Dioxide (NO$_2$)
Tianjin	94	62	43	Dimapur	130	n.a.	15
Yinchuan	92	49	25	Shimla	126	7	16
Shanghai	88	55	54	Bhubaneswar	117	5	13
Guiyang	85	55	23	Pondicherry	117	8	12
Hohhot	84	66	48	Aizawl	96	n.a.	11
Nanchang	83	54	34	Shillong	88	n.a.	12
Guangzhou	77	51	65	Thiruvananthapuram	76	7	25
Kunming	75	68	42				
Fuzhou	65	27	55	**AAQS**			
Nanning	64	59	48	China	100	60	40
Lhasa	57	7	25	EU	40	125*	40
Haikou	43	9	12	India	60	60	60
				US	150*	60	100
				WHO	20	20*	40

Notes: Data in the table refer to 2007 statistics for China and 2006 statistics for India. The ambient air quality standards (AAQS) set by each nation define the level of pollutants in the air that is considered to be harmful to public health and the environment. AAQS statistics in the table are obtained from relevant official webpages. There are three sets of AAQS in China; the lowest level (best air quality) is reported here. * refers to 24-hour average level.

Sources: NBS (2008) and CSO (2008a).

Another area is water pollution. For example, the two nations' main rivers are also at risk of being contaminated due to organic pollution. The main sources of water pollutants include domestic sewage, industrial effluents, and run-off from activities such as agricultural irrigation (which carries fertilizers and pesticides into groundwater). In China, on average, only 92% of the discharged industrial wastewater complies with the official standards according to the latest statistics (NBS, 2008). For some regions, this figure is very low, such as 29% in Tibet, 50% in Qinghai and 65% in Xinjiang. Incidentally, these regions are all located in the less developed western China, which is now rapidly catching up with the coastal area in terms of industrialization. Thus, environmental protection in western China should be strengthened so that the region will not follow the same development model as coastal China did with costly environmental damages. In major Indian cities, on average, about 19% of urban wastewater is discharged without treatment or collection (CSO, 2008a). In some cities such as Bhopal and Ludhiana, less than half of the wastewater is collected.[4] In China, the worst affected rivers in 2006 included Huang He, Songhuajiang, Huai He, Hai He and Liao He (Editorial Board, 2007). In India, Baitarani, Gandak, Godavari and Yamuna are some of the most polluted rivers.[5]

Over time, China's wastewater discharge has increased continuously, making it impossible for the economy to meet its target set in the 11th Five-Year Plan (Figure 7.1). However, the discharge of SO_2, chemical oxygen demand (COD) and soot has shown a flat or declining trend over time; therefore, it seems that the 11th Five-Year Plan targets for these pollutants could be met according to Figure 7.1. In India, between the late 1990s and recent years, there is evidence which shows a decline in the level of SO_2 in the air in major cities such as Ahmedabad, Bangalore, Chennai, Delhi, Hyderabad, Kolkata and Mumbai.[6] However, the level of NO_2

---

[4] For details, refer to Table 6.1.16, CSO (2008a).
[5] For details, refer to Table 6.1.17(b), CSO (2008a).
[6] According to Table 4.1.8, CSO (2008a).

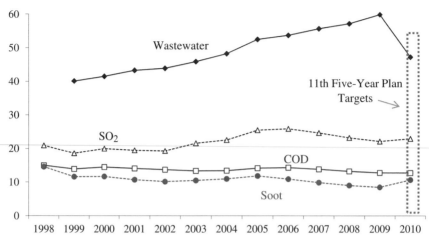

Figure 7.1   China: Total Waste Discharged, 1998–2010

Notes: The units are billion tons for wastewater and million tons for SO_2, COD and soot.
The numbers for 2010 are predicted targets.
Sources: NBS (2008, 2010) and MEP (2008).

increased significantly in Ahmedabad, Bangalore and Kolkata during the same period, while PM_{10} concentration in the air remained very high.[7] The national average indicators confirm the same trends in India: a declining concentration of SO_2, a modestly rising NO_2 level, and a stable but high concentration of particulate matter (PM_{10}) during the decade 1996–2005 (MEF, 2008).

7.2 Sources of Pollution

The industrial sector has been the main source of pollution in both countries, especially in China where this sector was responsible for 44.3% of wastewater discharged, 86.7% of sulfur dioxide emission and 78.3% of soot emission in the country in 2007 (NBS, 2008). Though India is less industrialized (than China), the country's industrial sector is expanding rapidly and has become a

---

[7] *Ibid.*

major source of pollutants discharged. This is particularly so in the more industrialized states such as Gujarat, Maharashtra, Tamil Nadu and Andhra Pradesh (MEF, 2001).

The poor air quality in Chinese and Indian cities is partly due to the expansion of the transport sector, especially the growth of motor vehicles. Over the past decade, the number of motor vehicles on the road has increased dramatically in both countries (Figure 7.2). This growth has been particularly strong in recent years. During 2005–2008, for instance, more than five million units were added to the roads every year in China (NBS, 2010). In 2009, this figure exceeded 12 million. The latest data from India also show that nearly one million units were added to the roads in Delhi during 2000–2004 (an increase from 3.4 million units in 2000 to 4.2 million units in 2004), and that the number of registered motor vehicles in Tamil Nadu rose from 4.6 million units to 8.6 million units during the same period.[8]

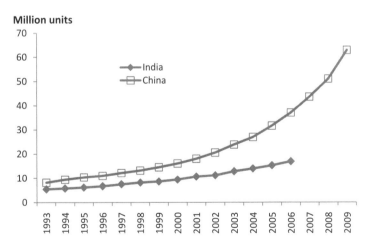

Figure 7.2   The Number of Motor Vehicles in China and India, 1993–2009

Sources: NBS (2010) and MORTH (2007).

---

[8] These figures are drawn from the website of Motor Transport Statistics, Ministry of Road Transport and Highways, Government of India (http://morth.nic.in).

The main polluting sectors in both countries are iron and steel, pulp and paper, petrochemical, mining, oil refinery and power generation, to cite a few. In particular, China's power generation sector accounts for about 60% of SO_2 and 23% of solid waste discharged in the industrial sector.[9] In addition, China's mining sector generates almost 40% of the country's industrial solid waste. In terms of wastewater discharge, the largest sectors in turn are pulp and paper, petrochemical and textile industries in China. In India, the iron and steel sector produces 87% of wastewater, 71% of metal air pollutants, and 32% of total air pollutants according to the estimates by Pandey (2005).

At the regional or state level, however, there is substantial variation. Among the Indian states, Pandey (2005) has identified the 12 largest polluters which generate over 70% of total industrial pollutants (toxic, metal, water, etc.).[10] In China, the top polluters are coastal and more industrialized regions such as Jiangsu, Guangdong, Shandong, Hebei and Zhejiang, which together account for over 40% of the country's industrial wastewater, air pollutants and solid waste.

7.3 Climate Change Responsibilities

From an international perspective, China and India are two of the world's largest carbon emitters and hence two major contributors to global climate change (Table 7.2). China was ranked the second largest emitter in 2006 and has probably overtaken the US to become the largest emitter in the world by the end of 2008. India's carbon emission exceeded Japan's in 2006 and is catching up with Russia's.

As per capita emission is still relatively low, especially in India, aggregate carbon emission is expected to increase in the

---

[9] These Chinese data are calculated using statistics from the NBS (2008).

[10] These states are Bihar, Madhya Pradesh, Maharashtra, Orissa, Andhra Pradesh, West Bengal, Uttar Pradesh, Punjab, Tamil Nadu, Gujarat, Karnataka and Rajasthan.

Table 7.2 CO_2 Emission and Intensity, 2006

Countries	Ranking	Total CO_2 (Mt)	World Shares (%)	CO_2 Per Head (t per capita)	CO_2 Per US\$ (t/US\$1)	CO_2 Per PPP\$ (kg/PPP\$1)
USA	1	5,697	20.34	19.00	0.51	0.51
China	2	5,607	20.02	4.27	2.68	0.65
Russia	3	1,587	5.67	11.14	4.25	1.08
India	4	1,250	4.46	1.13	1.78	0.34
Japan	5	1,213	4.33	9.49	0.24	0.34
Germany	6	823	2.94	10.00	0.41	0.37
Canada	7	539	1.92	16.52	0.64	0.53
UK	8	536	1.91	8.86	0.32	0.31
Korea	9	476	1.70	9.86	0.71	0.47
Italy	10	448	1.60	7.61	0.39	0.29
Iran	11	433	1.55	6.17	3.08	0.85
Mexico	12	416	1.49	3.97	0.63	0.40
Australia	13	394	1.41	19.02	0.82	0.62
France	14	377	1.35	5.97	0.26	0.22
Saudi Arabia	15	340	1.21	14.36	1.42	0.95
Indonesia	16	335	1.20	1.50	1.53	0.42
Top-16		20,471	73.10			
World		28,003	100.00	4.28	0.74	0.49

Notes: kg, t and Mt refer to kilogram, ton and million ton, respectively. CO_2 emissions are from fuel combustion only.
Source: IEA (2008).

near future in both China and India. In the long run, whether the two countries can achieve the goal of a fall in aggregate emission depends on the commitments of their governments. Between 1990 and 2005, most Organization for Economic Cooperation and Development (OECD) countries recorded a reduction in aggregate CO_2 emissions ranging from 71% in the UK to 8% in Turkey (OECD, 2007). The most significant reduction has been due to the fall in emissions from "mobile" sources (such as motor vehicles), which accounted for 69% and 54% of CO_2 emissions in the UK in 1990 and 2005, respectively.

However, as far as intensity is concerned, there is substantial scope for reduction. Emission intensity in China is one of the highest in the world, only behind Russia and Iran among the 16 top emitters in the world according to Table 7.2. Though India's emission intensity is well below China's, it was still higher than Indonesia's and Mexico's in 2006. Finally, it should be pointed out that the group ranking is slightly different if GDP is measured using international dollars, which is of course controversial (Table 7.2).

In terms of carbon emission per capita, the major developed economies can be divided into two camps, namely, the more emission-intensive and less emission-intensive economies. The former includes the US, Australia and Canada; while the latter is represented by Japan, France and the UK. The contrast between the two camps is that the former generates twice as much carbon emission as the latter. Whichever model China and India follow will have important implications for their own environment in general and global climate change in particular. Given the increasing environmental awareness domestically and the global campaign for climate change, China and India would probably have only one choice — to adopt a clean or cleaner development model.

7.4 Potential Policy Responses

Both China and India are in the process of industrialization and urbanization, which will add more pressure on the environment.

Due to both external demands and domestic conditions, the two countries thus have to take drastic actions to control pollution. Immediate actions can be taken to address these issues, such as energy efficiency, the transformation of economic and energy structures, and adoption of the world's best practice environmental regulations.

7.4.1 *Energy Efficiency*

Energy consumption is a main source of pollution, especially air pollution. Among the world's major economies, for example, the bulk of total CO_2 emissions comes from carbon emission due to energy consumption. Thus, energy efficiency directly affects emission intensity. According to Figure 7.3 which illustrates the relationship between energy consumption and income in 137 economies, it is obvious that China and India are outliers regardless of whether Japan or the US is used as the benchmark

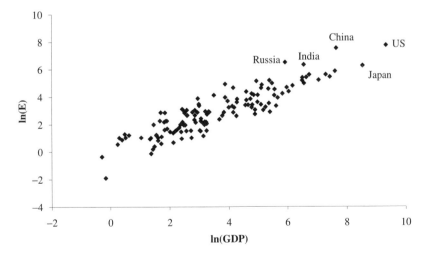

Figure 7.3   Energy Consumption and GDP in Selected Economies, 2006

Notes: The units are million tons of oil equivalent for energy consumption (E) and billions of US dollars for GDP.
Source: IEA (2008).

economy. As a matter of fact, in 2006, energy intensity defined as the amount of energy required per unit of GDP was 0.90 kgOE (kilogram of oil equivalent) in China and 0.80 kgOE in India. These efficiency scores are much higher than 0.21 kgOE in the US and 0.15 kgOE in Japan in the same year.[11] Therefore, there is scope for improvement in energy efficiency and, hence, reducing carbon emission intensity and slowing down the increase in aggregate emissions.

Energy structure is another important factor that influences the control of pollution, particularly air pollution. For decades, China and India have mainly relied on fossil fuel for energy. Nonfossil fuels (renewable, nuclear, hydro, etc.) have only had a small share over total energy consumption, i.e. 7.3% in China and 10.2% in India in 2007.[12] There is room for an increase in the use of cleaner energies such as natural gas and renewable energies. Among the OECD economies, the average share over primary energy consumption in 2007 was 22.6% for natural gas and 17.3% for renewable, nuclear, hydro and other alternative energies (IEA, 2008). In China, coal still accounted for 69.5% of total primary energy consumed in 2007. Though Indian coal consumption had a smaller share of 45.3% in the same year, this is still much higher than the OECD mean of 20.8% in 2007 (IEA, 2008). In the immediate future, new technologies should at least be adopted in coal mining and washing in both countries even though the consumption of coal cannot be reduced significantly.

7.4.2 *Environment-Friendly Development Model*

Traditionally, developed countries have followed a pollution-growth-clean model of development, which is now conceptualized in the popular environmental Kuznets curve (EKC). The latter implies that the degree of pollution and level of development

---

[11] These energy intensity statistics are drawn from the IEA (2008).

[12] These numbers are calculated using statistics from the NBS (2008) and CSO (2008b).

show an inverted-U shape. That is, pollution rises initially as an economy develops and then falls after economic development (normally measured by per capita income) reaches a certain level. This critical level of income is called the "turning point" in the literature. Over the past three decades, China has basically followed this traditional development trajectory. It is now time for the Chinese economy to undergo a structural transformation and for the Indian economy to adopt a more environment-friendly industrialization strategy. In fact, empirical research shows that the "turning point" income level is much lower in developing economies such as China than in the developed economies. This is called the "leapfrogging" factor or effect, which means developing countries can reach their turning points at an earlier stage of development. Wu (2010) found that China's turning point is 19,422 yuan (about US\$2,408 or PPP\$9,635 in 2007). Eleven out of 31 Chinese administrative regions reached this level of income per capita in 2007 and hence can afford to spend money on pollution control.[13] While there is no empirical evidence yet, Indian states could reach their "turning point" at different times, implying that some states could take actions first. For instance, during the 2005/2006 financial year, per capita income in India's more developed states or union territories was about US\$1,925 in Chandigarh, US\$1,558 in Goa and US\$1,371 in Delhi. These figures are still below the derived "turning point" income in China.[14]

In the case of China, the structural transformation of the economy implies the expansion of the service sector and development of high-technology and knowledge-intensive industries. China's service sector development is lagging behind, and hence

---

[13] These regions include Shanghai (66,367 yuan), Beijing (58,204 yuan), Tianjin (46,122 yuan), Zhejiang (37,411 yuan), Jiangsu (33,928 yuan), Guangdong (33,151 yuan), Shandong (27,807 yuan), Fujian (25,908 yuan), Liaoning (25,729 yuan), Inner Mongolia (25,393 yuan) and Hebei (19,877 yuan). Data are drawn from the NBS (2008).

[14] These statistics are calculated using data from the RBI (2008).

hinders the structural transformation of the economy. In 2007, for example, services accounted for 40.1% of China's GDP, which is much smaller than 53% in India, 64% in Brazil and 71% in Mexico, not to mention 75% in the UK and 76% in the US (NBS, 2008; World Bank, 2008). Though the service sector is relatively large in India, it is still dominated by the traditional services (Wu, 2007). In addition, there is also considerable variation across Indian states. The share of service sector value-added over gross state product (GSP) ranged from approximately 85% (the highest) in Chandigarh to approximately 38% (the lowest) in Jharkhand during the 2005/2006 financial year (RBI, 2008). Therefore, Indian policy focus should be on the promotion of modern services such as finance, IT and healthcare. Moreover, the Indian manufacturing sector has yet to take off. Policy makers should carefully monitor the activities of pollution-intensive sectors and the production of pollution-intensive products at both national and state levels.

7.4.3 *Environmental Regulations*

Environmental regulation plays an important role in pollution control. China and India can do much more to implement more stringent regulations and ensure better enforcement. A series of laws and regulations were promulgated in both countries in the 1980s (Table 7.3). There is, however, ample evidence which

Table 7.3 Selected Laws and Regulations Promulgated in China and India

Laws/Acts	India	China
Ocean Act		1982
Water Act	1974	1984
Air Act	1981	1987
Environment Law	1986	1989
Hazardous Waste Rules	1989	

Source: Author's own compilation.

shows the inadequacy and lack of enforcement of appropriate environmental regulations. In the case of India, Roychowdhury *et al.* (2006) argue that emissions from motor vehicles could be reduced by implementing an effective vehicle inspection and maintenance system, improving public transport services and controlling the explosive growth of private vehicles using proper tax policies. These authors also present New Delhi, the capital city of India, as a case study. Stringent regulations in the form of tough emission standards, a ban on diesel cars and so on have led to an improvement in ambient air quality in New Delhi (though the city is still far away from the clean air goal).

In China, during the 2008 Olympic Games, most cars in Beijing were banned from the roads and factories were closed temporarily. These actions resulted in a dramatic improvement in the quality of air during the Games. While these actions may be controversial, they do remind us that a decrease in vehicular and industrial emissions does significantly reduce the amount of pollutants discharged into the atmosphere and hence improve ambient air quality in urban areas. Thus, what Chinese authorities may do is to implement more stringent regulations instead of administrative orders. For example, to force structural transformation, regulations could target heavily polluted sectors and products that should either be reduced gradually or adopt cleaner technologies.

7.5 Conclusion

Whilst spectacular, economic growth in China and India has serious environmental consequences. One of these consequences is pollution, which is the topic of this chapter. Pollution has led to poor urban air quality, which is almost life-threatening in some cities in both China and India. It is shown that industrial sector and motor vehicular emissions are the main sources of air pollution. There is, however, variation among the regions or states as well as across the sectors in the two economies. From an international perspective, China and India are two of the largest carbon emitters in the world. The two giants' emission intensities (the amount of carbon emissions discharged per unit of output) are relatively high, implying the potential for improvement and for catch-up with the world's advanced economies. Whether China and India follow a more or less emission-intensive development model has important implications for the environment, both domestically and globally.

The policy recommendation in this chapter is to enhance energy efficiency and promote changes in energy consumption patterns and economic structure so as to adopt an environment-friendly development model in both countries. In addition, both governments should implement more stringent environmental regulations as well as strengthen their enforcement. As for the transformation of economic structure, China has an advantage over India: in the midst of the current US financial crisis, the Chinese government initiated a large stimulus package. Ideally, part of this fund should be spent on industrial upgrading and the improvement of energy efficiency.

Chapter 8

Conclusion

China and India have the world's most dynamic economies this century, and are expected to restore their prominence in the world economy centuries ago (see Figure 1.1, Chapter 1). Understanding these two economies will keep economists and other analysts occupied for generations. This book has presented a glimpse at some key topics which are by no means exhaustive. I hope many issues raised and discussed in this book can lead to further debates and research in this field. To conclude this book, the major findings are highlighted first in Section 8.1. Some further remarks are then presented in Section 8.2.

8.1 The Main Findings

This book contains six core chapters. Several major findings are highlighted here. First, it is found that recent high economic growth in China and India is mainly driven by productivity growth and fast accumulation of capital. This finding has important policy implications. On the one hand, the positive role of productivity in economic growth implies the possibility of sustained growth in the future. There is, however, considerable scope for improvement. Thus, productivity growth should be promoted and enhanced. On the other hand, at the current stage of development, investment still plays a vital role in maintaining high economic growth in the two countries. It is even more important in India. The economic growth gap between China and India is reflected in the rates of growth in capital formation in the two economies. While China's growth rate of capital formation has pretty much peaked, there is ample room for growth in India. Whether India can catch up with China to some extent depends on the level of investment that India can attain in the coming decades.

Second, substantial regional disparity exists in both countries. Nowadays it is more serious in China than in India. In particular, China's coastal areas led by the three autonomous municipalities (Shanghai, Beijing and Tianjin) are much better developed than the country's interior areas. It is found that, apart from favorable government policies, several region-specific factors also affect development in the various regions. These factors include urbanization, infrastructure, economic openness and human capital. Therefore, specific government policies should be implemented to address those issues in both China and India.

Third, over the past few decades, services have played very different roles in economic growth in the two Asian giants. From an international perspective, China's service sector development is lagging behind other economies at a similar stage of development while India's is well above the world trend. Thus, China has to expand its service sector so that the country's economic growth and job creation will not have to rely overwhelmingly on the manufacturing sector, which has been the source of rapid resource depletion and environmental damages in the country. In India, growth in services occurs mainly in the niche areas which are skill- and capital-intensive, and hence may not be able to create enough jobs for rural workers who are less educated. India therefore needs a "manufacturing revolution" like the service one which has taken place in recent decades.

Fourth, a common feature in recent economic growth in the two Asian giants is that pro-trade policies are supported and well exploited in both countries. As a result, exporting activities have played an important role in economic growth in China and India, especially in China, in recent decades. However, as two large economies in Asia, China and India have not traded bilaterally as much as they should even though the volume of trade between the two countries has grown. In terms of the patterns of trade, the two countries complement each other in some areas. There is considerable scope to remove barriers to bilateral trade and hence to fully explore the potential for trade between the two countries. The ongoing talks regarding a free trade agreement between the two governments are an important step towards the expansion of bilateral trade, though it may involve a long process of negotiations.

Finally, both China and India have to resolve many serious issues associated with energy consumption and environmental protection during the course of economic development. Economic growth can be costly to the environment and is not sustainable if the right environmental protection policies are not put in place. In particular, important lessons can be learned from the experience of three-decade rapid growth in coastal China. For China, the development of the country's interior regions can follow a different model that is environment-friendly and technology-intensive. India can also learn from China's experience and try to avoid the problems that Chinese policy makers are facing nowadays. In terms of energy consumption, carbon emission and environmental regulations, the major economies in the world have exhibited different models of development. Some are relatively green with low energy and emission intensities; others are at the opposite extreme. Whichever model China and India will follow has important implications for the world's resources and environment in the coming decades.

8.2 Growth Outlook in China and India

In the literature on the comparison of economic growth in China and India, one question is frequently asked: what is the potential for growth in China and India, particularly in China (where high growth took off a decade earlier than in India)? To conclude the book, this section briefly sheds some light on the growth outlook in the two economies.

According to endogenous growth theories, the potential for growth in an economy depends upon the role of productivity growth or technological progress (Romer, 1986; Lucas, 1988). Chapter 2 of this book has shown that total factor productivity (TFP) growth in both China and India has made a positive contribution to economic growth in the past few decades. Thus, the two economies are following the right trajectory towards sustained growth. There is currently a gap between the Asian giants and the major developed economies in the world in terms of TFP contribution to economic growth, with the giants lagging behind. By catching up, however, it is anticipated that TFP growth will play a more important role in economic growth in the two countries. This would be good news for sustainable growth in China and India in the coming decades.

A comparison of China and India with two other major East Asian countries, namely, South Korea and Japan, can also shed some light on the growth potential of the two giants. Figure 8.1 illustrates that, after economic takeoff, Japan and South Korea maintained high economic growth continuously for decades. On the one hand, the South Korean economy achieved an average rate of growth of 7.7% for four decades (1963–2002), though the world economy was interrupted by two oil crises and South Korea was severely hit by the 1997 Asian financial meltdown. Economic growth in South Korea has only slowed down in recent years, with an average rate of growth of 3.8% during 2003–2010.[1] In 2003, per capita GDP in South Korea was US$12,764.[2] On the other hand, the Japanese economy enjoyed a high rate of growth until 1973, when the first oil crisis occurred. By then, Japan's GDP per capita had reached US$19,343.[3] During the decade 1981–1990, per capita GDP in

---

[1] The growth rates and other statistics in this section are based on the latest World Development Indicators (http://www.worldbank.org), unless stated otherwise.

[2] 2000 constant prices.

[3] 2000 constant prices.

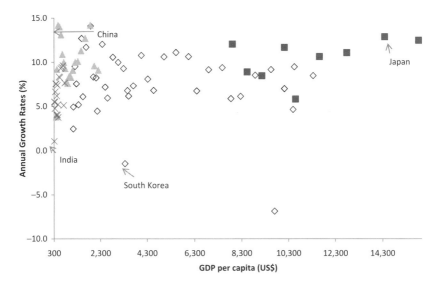

Figure 8.1 Growth and Income Per Capita in Four Asian Economies

Notes: Data are drawn from the World Development Indicators online database (http://www.worldbank.org), and cover the period 1990–2009 for China and India, 1961–2000 for South Korea and 1961–1969 for Japan.

Japan rose from US$23,361 to US$33,595, and the Japanese economy still maintained an average rate of growth of 4.6% annually. In 2009, per capita GDP was US$2,206 in China and US$757 in India.[4] Thus, even following a similar growth path as South Korea and Japan, China and India can maintain high growth for several more decades.

The process of transition from high to low growth in China and India will probably last longer than that undergone by the economies of Japan and South Korea. One major factor is the existence of large regional disparity in China and India. Economic growth often takes off in one region, such as the coastal region, and then spills over into the interior region and finally the entire nation. With continental-size economies like China and India, however, the process of regional growth

---

[4] 2000 constant prices.

spillovers will take much longer than it does in smaller countries such as Japan and South Korea.

A similar process of economic development across countries was popularized by the proposal of the so-called "flying geese" paradigm (Akamatsu, 1962; Ozawa, 2005). In Asia, high economic growth initially occurred in Japan in the 1950s and 1960s. As the Japanese growth slowed down, the four East Asian Tigers — South Korea, Taiwan, Hong Kong and Singapore — took over to enjoy high growth in the 1970s and 1980s, followed by Southeast Asian economies in the 1980s and 1990s. China and India have subsequently surpassed other major Asian economies to record high growth in the 1990s and 2000s.

However, in the context of China and India, apart from joining the international "flying geese" pattern, they have their own internal "flying geese" paradigm to be completed. In China, the coastal area has forged ahead in the last three decades; high growth will eventually spill over into the middle and western areas in the coming decades. In India, high growth has so far been associated with relatively rich, urbanized and industrialized states (Sachs *et al.*, 2002; Bhattacharya and Sakthivel, 2004); such growth has yet to spread to relatively poor, landlocked states. The process of a "flying geese"-type transition internally will take decades in both countries. These factors will make it possible to maintain high growth in China and India over the coming decades.

Bibliography

Abramovitz, Moses (1986). "Catching Up, Forging Ahead, and Falling Behind". *Journal of Economic History* 46(2), 385–406.

ADB (2004). *Key Indicators 2004* (online database). Asian Development Bank (http://www.adb.org/statistics).

ADB (2005). *Key Indicators 2005* (online database). Asian Development Bank (http://www.adb.org/statistics).

Akamatsu, K. (1962). "A Historical Pattern of Economic Growth in Developing Countries". *Journal of Developing Economies* 1(1), 3–25.

Baark, Erik and Jon Sigurdson (eds.) (1981). *India–China Comparative Research: Technology and Science for Development*. London: Curzon Press.

Balasubramanyam, V.N. and Y. Wei (2005a). "Textile and Clothing Exports from India and China: A Comparative Analysis". *Journal of Chinese Economic and Business Studies* 3(1), 23–37.

Balasubramanyam, V.N. and Y. Wei (2005b). "Foreign Direct Investment in India and China: A Comparative Study". Paper presented at the "Dynamic China: Past, Present and Future" International Conference, Chongqing University, Chongqing, March 31–April 1.

Barro, Robert J. and X. Sala-i-Martin (1995). *Economic Growth*. New York: McGraw-Hill Inc.

Benhabib, J. and M. Spiegel (1994). "The Role of Human Capital in Economic Development: Evidence from Aggregate Cross-Country Data". *Journal of Monetary Economics* 34, 143–174.

Bergmann, T. (1977). *The Development Models of India, the Soviet Union and China: A Comparative Analysis*. Assen: Van Gorcum.

Bhagwati, Jagdish (1984). "Splintering and Disembodiment of Services and Developing Nations". *The World Economy* 7(2), 133–143.

Bhalla, A.S. (1995). *Uneven Development in the Third World: A Study of China and India*. Basingstoke and New York: Macmillan/St. Martin's Press.

Bhanumurthy, N.R. and Arup Mitra (2004). "Economic Growth, Poverty, and Inequality in Indian States in the Pre-Reform and Reform Periods". *Asian Development Review* 21(2), 79–99.

Bhattacharya, B.B. and S. Sakthivel (2004). "Regional Growth and Disparity in India: Comparison of Pre- and Post-Reform Decades". *Economic and Political Weekly* 39(10), 1071–1077.

Bosworth, Barry and Susan M. Collins (2003). "The Empirics of Growth: An Update". Unpublished paper, Brookings Institution, Washington, D.C.

Brown, A.J. (1949). *Applied Economics: Aspects of World Economy in War and Peace*. London: George Allen and Unwin.

Brulhart, M. (1994). "Marginal Intra-Industry Trade: Measurement and the Relevance for the Pattern of Industrial Adjustment". *Weltwirtschaftliches Archiv* 130(3), 600–613.

Canning, David (1998). "A Database for the World Stocks of Infrastructure, 1950–95". *World Bank Economic Review* 12, 529–547.

Chanda, Rupa (2002). *Globalization of Services: India's Opportunities and Constraints*. New Delhi: Oxford University Press.

Chen, K.I. and J.S. Uppal (1971). *Comparative Development of India and China*. New York: Free Press.

Chow, Gregory (1993). "Capital Formation and Economic Growth in China". *Quarterly Journal of Economics* 108, 809–842.

Chow, Gregory and Kui-Wai Li (2002). "China's Economic Growth: 1952–2010". *Economic Development and Cultural Change* 51, 247–256.

CIA (2010). *2010 CIA World Factbook*. Langley, VA: Central Intelligence Agency, US Government.

Crompton, Paul and Yanrui Wu (2005). "Energy Consumption in China: Past Trends and Future Directions". *Energy Economics* 27, 195–208.

CSO (2005). *Online Database*. National Accounts Division, Central Statistical Organisation, Ministry of Statistics and Programme Implementation, Government of India (http://mospi.nic.in).

CSO (2006). *Selected Socioeconomic Statistics India 2006* (online database). Central Statistical Organisation, Ministry of Statistics and Programme Implementation, Government of India (http://mospi.nic.in).

CSO (2008a). *Compendium of Environmental Statistics 2007* (online database). Central Statistical Organisation, Ministry of Statistics and Programme Implementation, Government of India (http://mospi.nic.in).

CSO (2008b). *Energy Statistics 2007* (online database). Central Statistical Organisation, Ministry of Statistics and Programme Implementation, Government of India (http://mospi.nic.in).

Dalum, B., K. Laursen and G. Villumsen (1998). "Structural Change in OECD Export Specialisation Patterns: De-Specialisation and 'Stickiness'". *International Review of Applied Economics* 12(3), 423–444.

Das, Dilip K. (2006). *China and India: A Tale of Two Economies.* Abingdon: Routledge.

Démurger, S., J. Sachs, W.T. Woo, S. Bao, G. Chang and A. Mellinger (2002). "Geography, Economic Policy and Regional Development in China". *Asian Economic Papers* 1(1), 146–197.

Desai, Meghnad (2003). "India and China: An Essay in Comparative Political Economy". Paper presented at the IMF Conference on India and China, Delhi, November.

Dougherty, C. and D.W. Jorgenson (1996). "International Comparisons of the Sources of Economic Growth". *American Economic Review* 86(2), 25–29.

Dougherty, Sean and Vittorio Valli (2009). "China's Economy, India's Economy, Comparative Development". *European Journal of Comparative Economics* 6(1), 53–55.

Dzever, Sam and Jacques Jaussaud (eds.) (1999). *China and India: Economic Performance and Business Strategies of Firms in the Mid-1990s.* Basingstoke and New York: Macmillan/St. Martin's Press.

Easterly, W. and H. Yu (2000). "Global Development Network Growth Database". Unpublished paper, World Bank, Washington, D.C.

Economic Survey 2004–2005 (2005). Union Budget & Economic Survey, Ministry of Finance, Government of India (http://indiabudget.nic.in).

Editorial Board (2007). *China Environment Yearbook 2007*. Beijing: Xinhua Press.

Edwards, S. (1992). "Trade Orientation, Distortions and Growth in Developing Countries". *Journal of Development Economics* 39, 31–57.

Etienne, G., J. Astier, H. Bhushan and D. Zhong (1992). *Asian Crucible: The Steel Industry in China and India*. Newbury Park, CA: Sage.

Fan, Shenggen and Xiaobo Zhang (2002). "Production and Productivity Growth in Chinese Agriculture: New National and Regional Measures". *Economic Development and Cultural Change* 50(4), 819–838.

Fan, Shenggen, Xiaobo Zhang and Sherman Robinson (2003). "Structural Change and Economic Growth in China". *Review of Development Economics* 7(3), 360–377.

Farrell, Diana, Tarun Khanna, Jayant Sinha and Jonathan R. Woetzel (2004). "China and India: The Race to Growth". *McKinsey Quarterly*, Special Edition: China Today (http://www.mckinsey quarterly.com).

Franda, Marcus F. (2002). *China and India Online: Information Technology Politics and Diplomacy in the World's Two Largest Nations*. Oxford: Rowman & Littlefield Publishers, Inc.

Gordon, James and Poonam Gupta (2004). "Understanding India's Services Revolution". IMF Working Paper WP/04/171, International Monetary Fund, Washington, D.C.

Greenaway, D., R.C. Hine, C. Milner and R. Elliott (1994). "Adjustment and the Measurement of Marginal Intra-Industry Trade". *Weltwirtschaftliches Archiv* 130(2), 418–427.

Grossman, G. and A. Krueger (1995). "Economic Growth and the Environment". *Quarterly Journal of Economics* 110(2), 352–377.

Grubel, H. and P.J. Lloyd (1975). *Intra-Industry Trade*. London: Macmillan.

Guha-Khasnobis, Basudeb and Faisal Bari (2003). "Sources of Growth in South Asian Countries". In Isher Judge Ahluwalia and John Williamson (eds.), *The South Asian Experience with Growth*, New Delhi: Oxford University Press, Chapter 2.

Gupta, Chandra Prakash (1998). "India (1)". In *Improving Productivity in Service Sector*, Tokyo: Asian Productivity Organization.

Hamilton, C. and P. Kniest (1991). "Trade Liberalization, Structural Adjustment and Intra-Industry Trade". *Weltwirtschaftliches Archiv* 127(2), 356–367.

Harris, N. (1974). *India–China: Underdevelopment and Revolution*. Delhi: Vikas Publishing House.

Harrison, A. (1996). "Openness and Growth: A Time-Series, Cross-Country Analysis for Developing Countries". *Journal of Development Economics* 48, 419–447.

Hill, Richard and Kuniko Fujita (1995). "Product Cycles and International Divisions of Labor: Contrasts Between the United States and Japan". In David Smith and Jozsef Borocz (eds.), *A New World Order? Global Transformations in the Late Twentieth Century*, Westport, CT and London: Greenwood Press, pp. 91–108.

Holslag, Jonathan (2010). *China and India: Prospects for Peace*. New York: Columbia University Press.

Hsieh, Chang-Tai and Peter J. Klenow (2009). "Misallocation and Manufacturing TFP in China and India". *Quarterly Journal of Economics* 124(4), 1403–1448.

Hu, Zuliu F. and Mohsin S. Khan (1997). "Why Is China Growing So Fast?". *IMF Staff Papers* 44(1), 103–131.

Huang, Y. and T. Khanna (2003). "Can India Overtake China?". *Foreign Policy* 137, 74–81.

IEA (2007). *World Energy Outlook 2007: China and India Insights*. Paris: International Energy Agency.

IEA (2008). *Key World Energy Statistics 2008*. Paris: International Energy Agency.

IMF (2005). *World Economic Outlook 2005* (online database). International Monetary Fund (http://www.imf.org).

Jha, R. (2004). "The Political Economy of Recent Economic Growth in India". ASARC Working Paper 2004/12, Australia South Asia Research Centre, Australian National University, Canberra.

Jha, R. (ed.) (2005). *Economic Growth, Economic Performance and Welfare in South Asia*. Basingstoke and New York: Palgrave Macmillan.

Jian, T., J.D. Sachs and A.M. Warner (1996). "Trends in Regional Inequality in China". *China Economic Review* 7, 1–21.

Jiang, Xiaozhuan (ed.) (2004). *Service Industry in China: Growth and Structure*. Beijing: Social Sciences Documentation Publishing House.

Kalirajan, Kaliappa and Ulaganathan Sankar (eds.) (2003). *Economic Reform and the Liberalisation of the Indian Economy*. Cheltenham: Edward Elgar Publishing.

Kanbur, Ravi and Xiaobo Zhang (2005). "Fifty Years of Regional Inequality in China: A Journey Through Central Planning, Reform, and Openness". *Review of Development Economics* 9(1), 87–106.

Kehal, H.S. (ed.) (2005). *Foreign Investment in Rapidly Growing Countries: The Chinese and Indian Experiences*. Basingstoke and New York: Palgrave Macmillan.

Kim, Jong-Il and Lawrence Lau (1994). "The Sources of Economic Growth of the East Asian Newly Industrialized Countries". *Journal of the Japanese and International Economies* 8, 235–271.

Knight, John, Shi Li and Renwei Zhao (2004). "Divergent Means and Convergent Inequality of Incomes Among the Provinces and Cities of Urban China". Research Paper No. 2004/52, World Institute for Development Economics Research, Helsinki.

Kojima, K. (1964). "The Pattern of International Trade Among Advanced Countries". *Hitotsubashi Journal of Economics* 5(1), 16–36.

Korhonen, Pekka (1994). "The Theory of the Flying Geese Pattern of Development and Its Interpretations". *Journal of Peace Research* 31(1), 93–108.

Krugman, Paul (1994). "The Myth of Asia's Miracle". *Foreign Affairs* 73(6), 62–78.

Kuznets, S. (1971). *Economic Growth of Nations*. Cambridge, MA: Harvard University Press.

Laursen, K. (1998). "Revealed Comparative Advantage and the Alternatives as Measures of International Specialisation". DRUID Working Paper No. 98-30, Danish Research Unit for Industrial Dynamics, Copenhagen Business School, Copenhagen.

Li, Jiangfan (ed.) (2004a). *The Economic Analysis of China's Tertiary Sector I*. Guangzhou: Guangdong People's Press.

Li, Jiangfan (ed.) (2004b). *The Economic Analysis of China's Tertiary Sector II*. Guangzhou: Guangdong People's Press.

Li, Jingwen, Feihong Gong and Yisheng Zheng (1995). "Productivity and China's Economic Growth, 1953–1990". In K.Y. Tsui, T.T. Hsueh and Thomas G. Rawski (eds.), *Productivity, Efficiency and Reform in China's Economy*, Hong Kong: Chinese University Press.

Li, Shantong and Yongzhi Hou (eds.) (2003). *China's WTO Accession and Service Trade*. Beijing: Shangwu Press.

Li, Shantong, Yongzhi Hou, Yunzhong Liu and Jianwu He (2006). "Growth Prospects During 2006–2020". In Yanrui Wu (ed.), *Economic Transition, Growth and Globalization in China*, Cheltenham and Northampton, MA: Edward Elgar Publishing.

Lin, J. Yifu (1992). "Rural Reforms and Agricultural Growth in China". *American Economic Review* 82, 34–51.

Lucas, Robert E., Jr. (1988). "On the Mechanics of Economic Development". *Journal of Monetary Economics* 22(1), 3–42.

Luo, Yadong (2001). *China's Service Sector: A New Battlefield for International Corporations*. Copenhagen: Copenhagen Business School Press.

Maddison, A. (1998). *Chinese Economic Performance in the Long Run*. Paris: OECD Development Centre.

Maddison, A. (2003). *The World Economy: Historical Statistics*. Paris: OECD.

McManus, John, Mingzhi Li and Deependra Moitra (2007). *China and India: Opportunities and Threats for the Global Software Industry*. Oxford: Chandos Publishing.

McMillan, J., J. Whalley and L. Zhu (1989). "The Impact of China's Economic Reforms on Agricultural Productivity Growth". *Journal of Political Economy* 97(4), 781–807.

MEF (2001). *India: State of the Environment 2001*. Ministry of Environment & Forests, Government of India (http://envfor.nic.in).

MEF (2008). *Annual Report 2007/2008*. Ministry of Environment & Forests, Government of India (http://envfor.nic.in).

MEP (2008). *Statistical Communiqué of China's Environmental Conditions*. Beijing: Ministry of Environmental Protection.

Ministry of Labour and Employment (2010). *Annual Report to the People on Employment*. Government of India, July 1.

Mitra, A. (1992). "Growth and Poverty: The Urban Legend". *Economic and Political Weekly* 27(13), 659–665.

Mohan, Pratibha (1998). "India (2)". In *Improving Productivity in Service Sector*, Tokyo: Asian Productivity Organization.

Mooij, Jos (ed.) (2005). *The Politics of Economic Reforms in India*. New Delhi: Sage Publications India.

Morduch, J. and T. Sicular (2002). "Rethinking Inequality Decomposition with Evidence from Rural China". *The Economic Journal* 112, 93–106.

MORTH (2007). *Road Transport Yearbook 2006–07* (online database). Ministry of Road Transport & Highways, Government of India (http://morth.nic.in).

Mulder, Nanno (2001). "The Economic Performance of the Service Sector in Brazil, Mexico and the United States". In Robert M. Stern (ed.), *Services in the International Economy*, Ann Arbor: University of Michigan Press, pp. 185–210.

Nag, Barnali and Jyoti Parikh (2000). "Indicators of Carbon Emission Intensity from Commercial Energy Use in India". *Energy Economics* 22(4), 441–461.

Nagaraj, R., A. Varoudakis and M.A. Veganzones (2000). "Long-Run Growth Trends and Convergence Across Indian States". *Journal of International Development* 12(1), 45–70.

Naughton, Barry (1996). *Growing Out of the Plan: Chinese Economic Reform, 1978–1993*. Cambridge and New York: Cambridge University Press.

NBS (1997). *China Statistical Yearbook 1997*. National Bureau of Statistics. Beijing: China Statistics Press.

NBS (2004). *China Statistical Yearbook 2004*. National Bureau of Statistics. Beijing: China Statistics Press.

NBS (2006). *China Statistical Yearbook 2006*. National Bureau of Statistics. Beijing: China Statistics Press.

NBS (2008). *China Statistical Yearbook 2008*. National Bureau of Statistics. Beijing: China Statistics Press.

NBS (2010). *China Statistical Yearbook 2010*. National Bureau of Statistics. Beijing: China Statistics Press.

NBS (various issues). *China Statistical Yearbook*. National Bureau of Statistics. Beijing: China Statistics Press.

Negandhi, A.R. and P. Schran (eds.) (1990). *China and India: Foreign Investment and Economic Development*. Greenwich, CT: JAI Press.

Nehru, Vikram and Ashok Dhareshwar (1993). "A New Database on Physical Capital Stock: Sources, Methodology and Results". *Revista de Análisis Económico* 8(1), 37–59.

Ochel, Wolfgang and Manfred Wegner (1987). *Service Economies in Europe: Opportunities for Growth*. London and Boulder, CO: Pinter Publishers/Westview Press.

OECD (2005). *OECD in Figures, 2005 Edition* (online database). Organization for Economic Cooperation and Development (http://www.oecd.org).

OECD (2007). *OECD Environmental Data Compendium 2006/2007* (online database). Organization for Economic Cooperation and Development (http://www.oecd.org).

OECD (2010a). *OECD Factbook 2010: Economic, Environmental and Social Statistics* (online database). Organization for Economic Cooperation and Development (http://www.oecd.org).

OECD (2010b). *STAN Database for Structural Analysis* (online database). Organization for Economic Cooperation and Development (http://www.oecd.org).

Ono, Hisashi (2001). "Restructuring Strategy of Japan's Service Sector in the Twenty-First Century". In Seiichi Masuyama, Donna Vandenbrink and Chia Siow Yue (eds.), *Industrial Restructuring in East Asia*, Tokyo and Singapore: Nomura Research Institute/ Institute of Southeast Asian Studies.

Ozawa, T. (2005). *Institutions, Industrial Upgrading, and Economic Performance in Japan: The 'Flying-Geese' Paradigm of Catch-Up Growth*. Northampton, MA: Edward Elgar Publishing.

Pachauri, R.K. (2004). "The Future of India's Economic Growth: The Natural Resources and Energy Dimension". *Futures* 36, 703–713.

Panagariya, A. (2004). "India in the 1980s and 1990s: A Triumph of Reforms". IMF Working Paper WP/04/43, International Monetary Fund, Washington, D.C.

Pandey, Manish and Xiao-Yuan Dong (2009). "Manufacturing Productivity in China and India: The Role of Institutional Changes". *China Economic Review* 20(4), 754–766.

Pandey, Rita (2005). "Estimating Sectoral and Geographical Industrial Pollution Inventories in India: Implications for Using Effluent Charge Versus Regulation". *Journal of Development Studies* 41(1), 33–61.

Park, Se-Hark (1989). "Linkages Between Industry and Services and Their Implications for Urban Employment Generation in Developing Countries". *Journal of Development Economics* 30, 359–379.

Paul, Shyamal and Rabindra N. Bhattacharya (2004a). "Causality Between Energy Consumption and Economic Growth in India: A Note on Conflicting Results". *Energy Economics* 26, 977–983.

Paul, Shyamal and Rabindra N. Bhattacharya (2004b). "CO$_2$ Emission from Energy Use in India: A Decomposition Analysis". *Energy Policy* 32, 585–593.

Perkins, D. (1988). "Reforming China's Economic System". *Journal of Economic Literature* 26(2), 601–645.

Piketty, Thomas and Nancy Qian (2009). "Income Inequality and Progressive Income Taxation in China and India, 1986–2015". *American Economic Journal: Applied Economics* 1(2), 53–63.

Planning Commission (2005). *Mid-Term Appraisal of the Tenth Five Year Plan (2002–2007)*. Government of India (http://planning commission.nic.in).

Pritchett, L. (1997). "Where Has All the Education Gone?". Policy Research Working Paper No. 1551, World Bank, Washington, D.C.

Qin, Duo (2004). "Is the Rising Services Sector in the People's Republic of China Leading to Cost Disease?". ERD Working Paper No. 50, Asian Development Bank, Manila.

Raiser, M. (1998). "Subsidizing Inequality: Economic Reforms, Fiscal Transfers and Convergence Across Chinese Provinces". *Journal of Development Studies* 34, 1–26.

Rao, M.G., R.T. Shand and K.P. Kalirajan (1999). "Convergence of Incomes Across Indian States: A Divergent View". *Economic and Political Weekly* 34(13), 769–778.

Ravallion, M. and G. Datt (1996). "How Important to India's Poor Is the Sectoral Composition of Economic Growth?". *World Bank Economic Review* 10(1), 1–25.

RBI (2004). *Handbook of Statistics on the Indian Economy 2003/2004* (online database). Reserve Bank of India (http://www.rbi.org.in).

RBI (2005). *Handbook of Statistics on the Indian Economy 2004/2005* (online database). Reserve Bank of India (http://www.rbi.org.in).

RBI (2008). *Handbook of Statistics on the Indian Economy 2007/2008* (online database). Reserve Bank of India (http://www.rbi.org.in).

RBI (2009). *Handbook of Statistics on the Indian Economy 2008/2009* (online database). Reserve Bank of India (http://www.rbi.org.in).

RBI (2010). *Handbook of Statistics on the Indian Economy 2009/2010* (online database). Reserve Bank of India (http://www.rbi.org.in).

Renard, Mary-Francoise (ed.) (2002). *China and Its Regions: Economic Growth and Reform in Chinese Provinces*. Cheltenham: Edward Elgar Publishing.

Reynolds, Bruce L. (ed.) (1987). *Reform in China: Challenges and Choices*. New York: M.E. Sharpe.

Rodrik, Dani and Arvind Subramanian (2005). "From 'Hindu Growth' to Productivity Surge: The Mystery of the Indian Growth Transition". *IMF Staff Papers* 52(2), 193–228.

Romer, Paul M. (1986). "Increasing Returns and Long-Run Growth". *Journal of Political Economy* 94(5), 1002–1037.

Rosen, George (1992). *Contrasting Styles of Industrial Reform: China and India in the 1980s*. Chicago: University of Chicago Press.

Roychowdhury, A., V. Chattopadhyaya, C. Shah and P. Chandola (2006). *The Leapfrog Factor: Clearing the Air in Asian Cities*. New Delhi: Centre for Science and Environment.

Sachs, J.D., N. Bajpai and A. Ramiah (2002). "Understanding Regional Economic Growth in India". *Asian Economic Papers* 1(3), 32–62.

Sala-i-Martin, Xavier (1997). "I Just Ran Two Million Regressions". *American Economic Review* 87, 178–183.

Santos-Paulino, Amelia U. and Guanghua Wan (eds.) (2010). *The Rise of China and India: Impacts, Prospects and Implications*. Basingstoke: Palgrave Macmillan.

Selden, T.M. and D. Song (1994). "Environmental Quality and Development: Is There a Kuznets Curve for Air Pollution Emission?". *Journal of Environmental Economics and Management* 27, 147–162.

Shalizi, Zmarak (2007). "Energy and Emission". In L. Alan Winters and Shahid Yusuf (eds.), *Dancing with Giants: China, India and the Global Economy*, Washington, D.C.: World Bank.

Shanker, Daya, I.K.M. Mokhtarul Wadud and Harminder Singh (2009). "A Comparative Study of Banking in China and India: Non-Performing Loans and the Level Playing Field". *Indian Economic Journal* 57(3), 118–138.

Shirai, Sayuri (2002). "Banking Sector Reforms in India and China: Does India's Experience Offer Lessons for China's Future Reform Agenda?". *Asia-Pacific Development Journal* 9(2), 51–82.

Singh, Swaran (2005). "China–India Economic Engagement: Building Mutual Confidence". CSH Occasional Paper No. 10, Centre de Sciences Humaines, French Research Institutes in India, New Delhi.

Sinha, Swapna Sandesh (2007). *Comparative Analysis of FDI in China and India: Can Laggards Learn from Leaders?* Boca Raton, FL: Dissertation.com.

Soo, Kwok Tong (2005). "New Debates over Service Outsourcing to China and India". *Malaysian Journal of Economic Studies* 42(1–2), 63–67.

Srinivasan, T.N. (1994). *Agriculture and Trade in China and India: Policies and Performance Since 1950*. San Francisco, CA: ICS Press.

Srinivasan, T.N. (2004). "China and India: Economic Performance, Competition and Cooperation: An Update". *Journal of Asian Economics* 15, 613–636.

Srinivasan, T.N. (2005). "Comments on 'From Hindu Growth to Productivity Surge: The Mystery of the Indian Growth Transition'". *IMF Staff Papers* 52(2), 229–233.

Srivastava, Leena (1997). "Energy and CO_2 Emission in India: Increasing Trends and Alarming Portents". *Energy Policy* 25(11), 941–949.

Swamy, S. (1973). *Economic Growth in China and India, 1952–1970: A Comparative Appraisal*. Chicago: University of Chicago Press.

Swamy, S. (1989). *Economic Growth in China and India: A Perspective by Comparison*. New Delhi: Vikas.

Swamy, S. (2003). *Economic Reforms and Performance: China and India in Comparative Perspective*. New Delhi: Konark Publishers Pvt. Ltd.

Temple, J. (1998). "Robustness Tests of the Augmented Solow Model". *Journal of Applied Econometrics* 13, 361–375.

The Economist (2005). "A Survey of India and China". March 5.

Tseng, Wanda and David Cowen (eds.) (2005). *India's and China's Recent Experience with Reform and Growth*. Basingstoke: Palgrave Macmillan.

Wan, Guanghua (2004). "Accounting for Income Inequality in Rural China: A Regression-Based Approach". *Journal of Comparative Economics* 32, 348–363.

Wan, Guanghua and Amelia U. Santos-Paulino (2008). "The Rise of China and India: Growth, Trade, Investment and Institutional Developments — Introduction". *The World Economy* 31(10), 1273–1276.

WHO (2006). *WHO Air Quality Guidelines for Particulate Matter, Ozone, Nitrogen Dioxide and Sulfur Dioxide — Global Update 2005*. World Health Organization (http://www.who.int).

Wilson, D. and R. Purushothaman (2003). "Dreaming with BRICs: The Path to 2050". Global Economics Paper No. 99, Goldman Sachs, New York.

Winters, L. Alan and Shahid Yusuf (eds.) (2007). *Dancing with Giants: China, India and the Global Economy*. Washington, D.C.: World Bank.

Wirtz, Jochen (2000). "Growth of the Service Sector in Asia". *Singapore Management Review* 22(2), 37–54.

Wolfl, Anita (2005). "The Service Economy in OECD Countries". In *Enhancing the Performance of the Service Sector*, Paris: OECD.

Wong, John and Ruobing Liang (2003a). "China's Service Industry (I): Growth and Structural Change". EAI Background Brief No. 162, East Asian Institute, National University of Singapore, Singapore.

Wong, John and Ruobing Liang (2003b). "China's Service Industry (II): Gearing Up for WTO Challenges". EAI Background Brief No. 163, East Asian Institute, National University of Singapore, Singapore.

World Bank (1997). *China 2020: Development Challenges in the New Century*. Washington, D.C.: World Bank.

World Bank (2005). *World Development Indicators 2005* (online database). World Bank (http://www.worldbank.org).

World Bank (2008). *World Development Indicators 2008* (online database). World Bank (http://www.worldbank.org).

World Bank (2010). *World Development Indicators 2010* (online database). World Bank (http://www.worldbank.org).

Wu, Libo, Shinji Kaneko and Shunji Matsuoka (2006). "Dynamics of Energy-Related CO_2 Emission in China During 1980 to 2002: The Relative Importance of Energy Supply-Side and Demand-Side Effects". *Energy Policy* 34, 3549–3572.

Wu, Yanrui (2004). *China's Economic Growth: A Miracle with Chinese Characteristics*. London and New York: RoutledgeCurzon.

Wu, Yanrui (2006). "Changing Bilateral Trade and Implications for Free Trade Agreements in the Asian Pacific Region". In Abu Siddique (ed.), *Regionalism, Trade and Economic Development*, Cheltenham: Edward Elgar.

Wu, Yanrui (2007). "Service Sector Growth in China and India: A Comparison". *China: An International Journal* 5(1), 137–154.

Wu, Yanrui (2008). *Productivity, Efficiency and Economic Growth in China*. Basingstoke: Palgrave Macmillan.

Wu, Yanrui (2010). "Regional Environmental Performance and Its Determinants in China". *China & World Economy* 18(3), 73–89.

Wu, Yanrui and Zhangyue Zhou (2006). "Bilateral Trade Between China and India". *Journal of Asian Economics* 17(3), 509–518.

Xu, Y.C. (2004). *Electricity Reform in China, India and Russia: The World Bank Template and the Politics of Power*. Cheltenham: Edward Elgar.

Young, A. (1994). "Lessons from the East Asian NICs: A Contrarian View". *European Economic Review* 110, 641–680.

Zhang, Xiaobo and Kevin Zhang (2003). "How Does Globalization Affect Regional Inequality Within a Developing Country? Evidence from China". *Journal of Development Studies* 39, 47–67.

Zhou, Z.Y. (1997). *Effects of Grain Marketing Systems on Grain Production: A Comparative Study of China and India*. New York: Food Products Press.

Zhu, Jianhong (2005). "On Economic Aggregate and Structural Changes by the Chief of the National Bureau of Statistics". *People's Daily*, December 21, p. 5.

Zou, Gaolu and K.W. Chau (2006). "Short- and Long-Run Effects Between Oil Consumption and Economic Growth in China". *Energy Policy* 34, 3644–3655.

Index